VB6 AND WBEMSCRIPTING ASYNC

Working with ExecNotificationQueryAsync and __InstanceDeletionEvent

Richard Thomas Edwards

CONTENTS

IT CAN'T GET MUCH EASIER
THAN THIS
Let's dive right in

W HEN IT COMES RIGHT DOWN TO IT, THERE IS SOMETHNG SPECIAL
EVENT DRIVEN CODE THAT, IF FOR NO OTHER REASON, ASYNC CALLS
ARE MORE CHALLENGING THAN SYNC CALLS.

Truth is, there really isn't much to making the call work. It is more what you plan on doing with the information that makes the coding of an Async call fun and exciting to work with.

Your normal sync call -I'm not including the get value function, it takes the focus away from the basic logic – looks like this:

```
Set l = CreateObject("WbemScripting.SWbemLocator ")
Set svc = l.ConnectServer(".", "root\cimv2 ")
svc.Security_.AuthenticationLevel = 6
svc.Security_.ImpersonationLevel = 3
Set ob = svc.Get("Win32_Process ")
Set objs = ob.Instances_
```

And, at this point, we do our usual loops and hammer the output into submission.

The Async version of this looks like this:

```
Dim w
w = 0
Sub sink_OnCompleted(iHResult, objWbemErrorObject,
objWbemAsyncContext)

End Sub

Sub sink_OnObjectReady(objWbemObject,  objWbemAsyncContext)

    Set objs = objWbemObject.Instances_

    w=1
End Sub

Set l = CreateObject("WbemScripting.SWbemLocator ")
Set svc = l.ConnectServer(".", "root\cimv2 ")
svc.Security_.AuthenticationLevel = 6
svc.Security_.ImpersonationLevel = 3
Set mysink = WScript.CreateObject("WbemScripting.SWbemSink", "SINK_")
Call svc.ExecNotificationQueryAsync(mysink, "Select * From Win32_Process ")

Do While(w = 0)
    WScript.Sleep(500)
Loop
```

So, what is going on here? Well in the first place, I ran VB6, made a reference to The WMI Scripting Library and then created a withevents statement to create the two subs added above. (You don't think I remember this by heart do you?)

Next, I used WScript.CreateObject to create an instance of WbemScripting.SWbemSink and then used it to register my Sink event handler "Sink_".

I used Call – yes, it is still around – so that the "cannot use **parentheses while calling a sub**" dies a horrible death and the async event handler is added to the GetAsync call.

Then I used the you aren't going anywhere until I get an answer routine next with the Do While Loop.

Now, you're probably wondering why I just don't use the sink_OnCompleted sub to tell the Do While routine that we're done. It is because the sink_OnCompleted will not get called when you use get. Not in COM and not in .Net. Why? Because, the information you are wanting to get from the call isn't in the objWbemObject as a collection of objects at that level, it is in objWbemObject.Instances_ and therefore, you become the notification that you've completed the cycle..

A Full Async Example Using ExecQueryAsync

BELOW, IS A FULL ASYNC EXAMPLE.

```
Dim w
Dim tempstr
Dim strQuery

strQuery= "Select  *  From  __InstanceDeletionEvent  WITHIN  1  where
TargetInstance ISA 'Win32_Process'")

Function GetValue(ByVal Name, ByVal obj)

  Dim tempstr, pos, pName
  pName = Name
  tempstr = obj.GetObjectText_
  Name = Name + " = "
  pos = InStr(tempstr, Name)
  if pos Then
    pos = pos + Len(Name)
```

```vbscript
        tempstr = Mid(tempstr, pos, Len(tempstr))
        pos = InStr(tempstr, ";")
        tempstr = Mid(tempstr, 1, pos - 1)
        tempstr = Replace(tempstr, Chr(34), "")
        tempstr = Replace(tempstr, "{", "")
        tempstr = Replace(tempstr, "}", "")
        tempstr = Trim(tempstr)
        if len(tempstr) > 13 then
            if obj.Properties_(pName).CIMType = 101 Then
                tempstr = Mid(tempstr, 5, 2) + "/" + _
                Mid(tempstr, 7, 2) + "/" + _
                Mid(tempstr, 1, 4) + " " + _
                Mid(tempstr, 9, 2) + ":" + _
                Mid(tempstr, 11, 2) + ":" + _
                Mid(tempstr, 13, 2)
            End If
        End If
        GetValue = tempstr
    Else
        GetValue = ""
    End If

End Function

sub sink_OnObjectReady(objWbemObject, objWbemAsyncContext)
    Set obj = objWbemObject
        For Each prop in obj.Properties_
            Tempstr = Tempstr & prop.Name & " " & GetValue(prop.Name, obj) &
vbCrLf
        Next
    MsgBox (tempstr)
    Tempstr = ""
```

```
End Sub

w = 0

Set l = CreateObject("WbemScripting.SWbemLocator")
Set svc = l.ConnectServer(".", "root\CIMV2")
svc.Security_.AuthenticationLevel = 6
svc.Security_.ImpersonationLevel = 3

Set mysink = WScript.CreateObject("WBemScripting.SWbemSink", "sink_")
Call svc.ExecNotificationQueryAsync(mysink, strQuery)

Do While w = 0
  WScript.Sleep(500)
Loop
```

And the output is on the next page.

Caption System Idle Process
CommandLine
CreationClassName Win32_Process
CreationDate
CSCreationClassName Win32_ComputerSystem
CSName WIN-VNQ7KUKQ4NE
Description System Idle Process
ExecutablePath
ExecutionState
Handle 0
HandleCount 0
InstallDate
KernelModeTime 49024471250000
MaximumWorkingSetSize
MinimumWorkingSetSize
Name Win32_Process
OSCreationClassName Win32_OperatingSystem
OSName Microsoft Windows Server 2012 R2 Standard
Evaluation|C:\\Windows|\\Device\\Harddisk1\\Partition2
OtherOperationCount 0
OtherTransferCount 0
PageFaults 1
PageFileUsage 0
ParentProcessId 0
PeakPageFileUsage 0
PeakVirtualSize 65536
PeakWorkingSetSize 24
Priority 0
PrivatePageCount 0
ProcessId 0
QuotaNonPagedPoolUsage 0
QuotaPagedPoolUsage 0
QuotaPeakNonPagedPoolUsage 0
QuotaPeakPagedPoolUsage 0
ReadOperationCount 0
ReadTransferCount 0
SessionId 0
Status
TerminationDate
ThreadCount 8
UserModeTime 0
VirtualSize 65536
WindowsVersion 6.3.9600
WorkingSetSize 24
WriteOperationCount 0

OK

The logic behind using the Dictionary Object

Making the work easier to manage

A T THIS POINT, SINCE WE KNOW THE CODE WORKS, THE BIGGEST QUESTION SHOULD BE: HOW DO WE MAKE IT EASY TO WORK WITH AN IN A STYLE THAT MAKES SENSE? If you read the book on GetAsync, I showed you three ways the rendering logic could be used to generate reports and other forms of outputs presented in every book I write about WMI. I included and used arrays but warned the solution on using them was limited to the GetAsync routine.

There was a reason for this. A multi-dimensional array only needed to be re-dimensioned or re-dimmed only once. But that was because we knew how many objs were in the collection. In the case of ExecQueryAsync, we have no idea how many objs are in the collection because each object is being presented as a single object instead of a collection.

However, there are always exceptions to the rules and a single dimension row can accept a collection of Column values and be re-dimensioned dynamically and we're back with three possible ways of getting the job done.

With that said, what I would like to do here is show you the three different ways you can accomplish the same task:

In line

```
Dim Names()
Dim Values()

Dim x
Dim y

Dim strQuery
strQuery= "Select  *  From  __InstanceDeletionEvent  WITHIN  1  where
TargetInstance ISA 'Win32_Process'")

x=0
y=0

Function GetValue(ByVal Name, ByVal obj)

   Dim tempstr, pos, pName
   pName = Name
   tempstr = obj.GetObjectText_
   Name = Name + " = "
   pos = InStr(tempstr, Name)
   if pos Then
      pos = pos + Len(Name)
      tempstr = Mid(tempstr, pos, Len(tempstr))
      pos = InStr(tempstr, ";")
      tempstr = Mid(tempstr, 1, pos - 1)
      tempstr = Replace(tempstr, Chr(34), "")
      tempstr = Replace(tempstr, "{", "")
      tempstr = Replace(tempstr, "}", "")
      tempstr = Trim(tempstr)
      if len(tempstr) > 13 then
```

```vbscript
        if obj.Properties_(pName).CIMType = 101 Then
          tempstr = Mid(tempstr, 5, 2) + "/" + _
          Mid(tempstr, 7, 2) + "/" + _
          Mid(tempstr, 1, 4) + " " + _
          Mid(tempstr, 9, 2) + ":" + _
          Mid(tempstr, 11, 2) + ":" + _
          Mid(tempstr, 13, 2)
        End If
      End If
      GetValue = tempstr
      Else
      GetValue = ""
      End If

End Function

sub sink_OnObjectReady(objWbemObject, objWbemAsyncContext)

    Set obj = objWbemObject.Properties_.Item("TargetInstance").Value
    If y = 0 then
      txtstream.WriteLine("<tr>")
      For Each prop in obj.Properties_
        txtstream.WriteLine("<th>" & prop.Name & "</th>")
      Next
      txtstream.WriteLine("</tr>")
    End If

    txtstream.WriteLine("<tr>")
    For Each prop in obj.Properties_
      txtstream.WriteLine("<td>" & GetValue(prop.Name, obj) & "</td>")
    Next
    txtstream.WriteLine("</tr>")
    y=y+1
```

End Sub

Sub sink_OnCompleted(iHResult, objWbemErrorObject, objWbemAsyncContext)

    w = 1

End Sub

    w = 0

```
Set ws = CreateObject("WScript.Shell")
Set fso = CreateObject("Scripting.FileSystemObject")
Set txtstream = fso.OpenTextFile(ws.CurrentDirectory +
"\Win32_Process.html", 2, true, -2)
    txtstream.WriteLine("<html>")
    txtstream.WriteLine("<head>")
    txtstream.WriteLine("<style type='text/css'>")
    txtstream.WriteLine("th")
    txtstream.WriteLine("{")
    txtstream.WriteLine("   COLOR: darkred;")
    txtstream.WriteLine("   BACKGROUND-COLOR: white;")
    txtstream.WriteLine("   FONT-FAMILY:font-family: Cambria, serif;")
    txtstream.WriteLine("   FONT-SIZE: 12px;")
    txtstream.WriteLine("   text-align: left;")
    txtstream.WriteLine("   white-Space: nowrap;")
    txtstream.WriteLine("}")
    txtstream.WriteLine("td")
    txtstream.WriteLine("{")
    txtstream.WriteLine("   COLOR: navy;")
    txtstream.WriteLine("   BACKGROUND-COLOR: white;")
    txtstream.WriteLine("   FONT-FAMILY: font-family: Cambria, serif;")
```

```
txtstream.WriteLine("    FONT-SIZE: 12px;")
txtstream.WriteLine("    text-align: left;")
txtstream.WriteLine("    white-Space: nowrap;")
txtstream.WriteLine("}")
txtstream.WriteLine("</style>")
txtstream.WriteLine("<title>Win32_Process</title>")
txtstream.WriteLine("</head>")
txtstream.WriteLine("<body>")
txtstream.WriteLine("<table Border='1' cellpadding='1' cellspacing='1'>")
txtstream.WriteLine("<tr>")

Set l = CreateObject("WbemScripting.SWbemLocator")
Set svc = l.ConnectServer(".", "root\CIMV2")
svc.Security_.AuthenticationLevel = 6
svc.Security_.ImpersonationLevel = 3

Set mysink = WScript.CreateObject("WBemScripting.SWbemSink", "sink_")
Call svc.ExecNotificationQueryAsync(mysink, strQuery)

Do While w = 0
  WScript.Sleep(500)
Loop

txtstream.WriteLine("</table>")
txtstream.WriteLine("</body>")
txtstream.WriteLine("</html>")
txtstream.close
```

Using an Array of Arrays

```
Dim Names()
Dim Cols()
Dim Rows()
```

```vbscript
Dim x
Dim y

Dim strQuery

strQuery= "Select * From ___InstanceDeletionEvent WITHIN 1 where
TargetInstance ISA 'Win32_Process'")


x=0
y=0

Function GetValue(ByVal Name, ByVal obj)

    Dim tempstr, pos, pName
    pName = Name
    tempstr = obj.GetObjectText_
    Name = Name + " = "
    pos = InStr(tempstr, Name)
    if pos Then
        pos = pos + Len(Name)
        tempstr = Mid(tempstr, pos, Len(tempstr))
        pos = InStr(tempstr, ";")
        tempstr = Mid(tempstr, 1, pos - 1)
        tempstr = Replace(tempstr, Chr(34), "")
        tempstr = Replace(tempstr, "{", "")
        tempstr = Replace(tempstr, "}", "")
        tempstr = Trim(tempstr)
        if len(tempstr) > 13 then
            if obj.Properties_(pName).CIMType = 101 Then
                tempstr = Mid(tempstr, 5, 2) + "/" + _
                Mid(tempstr, 7, 2) + "/" + _
```

```vbnet
                Mid(tempstr, 1, 4) + " " + _
                Mid(tempstr, 9, 2) + ":" + _
                Mid(tempstr, 11, 2) + ":" + _
                Mid(tempstr, 13, 2)
        End If
      End If
      GetValue = tempstr
    Else
      GetValue = ""
    End If


End Function

sub sink_OnObjectReady(objWbemObject, objWbemAsyncContext)

    Set obj = objWbemObject.Properties_.Item("TargetInstance").Value
    x = 0
    if y = 0 then
      ReDim Names(obj.Properties_.Count)
      For Each prop in obj.Properties_
        Names(x) = prop.Name
        x=x+1
      Next
    End If


    x = 0
    ReDim Cols(obj.Properties_.Count)
    For Each prop in obj.Properties_
        Cols(x) = GetValue(prop.Name, obj)
        x=x+1
    Next
    ReDim Preserve Rows(y + 1)
    Rows(y) = Cols
```

```
        x = 0
        y= y+1

    End Sub

    Sub             sink_OnCompleted(iHResult,             objWbemErrorObject,
objWbemAsyncContext)

        w = 1

    End Sub


    w = 0

    Set ws = CreateObject("WScript.Shell")
    Set fso = CreateObject("Scripting.FileSystemObject")
    Set     txtstream     =     fso.OpenTextFile(ws.CurrentDirectory     +
"\Win32_Process.html", 2, true, -2)
    txtstream.WriteLine("<html>")
    txtstream.WriteLine("<head>")
    txtstream.WriteLine("<style type='text/css'>")
    txtstream.WriteLine("th")
    txtstream.WriteLine("{")
    txtstream.WriteLine("    COLOR: darkred;")
    txtstream.WriteLine("    BACKGROUND-COLOR: white;")
    txtstream.WriteLine("    FONT-FAMILY:font-family: Cambria, serif;")
    txtstream.WriteLine("    FONT-SIZE: 12px;")
    txtstream.WriteLine("    text-align: left;")
    txtstream.WriteLine("    white-Space: nowrap;")
    txtstream.WriteLine("}")
    txtstream.WriteLine("td")
    txtstream.WriteLine("{")
```

```
txtstream.WriteLine("    COLOR: navy;")
txtstream.WriteLine("    BACKGROUND-COLOR: white;")
txtstream.WriteLine("    FONT-FAMILY: font-family: Cambria, serif;")
txtstream.WriteLine("    FONT-SIZE: 12px;")
txtstream.WriteLine("    text-align: left;")
txtstream.WriteLine("    white-Space: nowrap;")
txtstream.WriteLine("}")
txtstream.WriteLine("</style>")
txtstream.WriteLine("<title>Win32_Process</title>")
txtstream.WriteLine("</head>")
txtstream.WriteLine("<body>")
txtstream.WriteLine("<table Border='1' cellpadding='1' cellspacing='1'>")
txtstream.WriteLine("<tr>")

Set l = CreateObject("WbemScripting.SWbemLocator")
Set svc = l.ConnectServer(".", "root\CIMV2")
svc.Security_.AuthenticationLevel = 6
svc.Security_.ImpersonationLevel = 3

Set mysink = WScript.CreateObject("WBemScripting.SWbemSink", "sink_")
Call svc.ExecNotificationQueryAsync(mysink, strQuery)

Do While w = 0
  WScript.Sleep(500)
Loop

for x = 0 To uBound(Names) -1
  txtstream.WriteLine("<th>" & Names(x)  & "</th>")
next
txtstream.WriteLine("</tr>")
for y = 0 to UBound(Rows) -1
  C = Rows(y)
  txtstream.WriteLine("<tr>")
```

```
    for x = 0 To uBound(Names) -1
        txtstream.WriteLine("<td>" & C(x) & "</td>")
    next
    txtstream.WriteLine("</tr>")
next

txtstream.WriteLine("</table>")
txtstream.WriteLine("</body>")
txtstream.WriteLine("</html>")
txtstream.close
```

Using the Dictionary Object

```
Dim dNames
Dim drows

Set dNames = CreateObject("Scripting.Dictionary")
Set dRows = CreateObject("Scripting.Dictionary")

Dim x
Dim y

Dim strQuery

strQuery= "Select * From ___InstanceDeletionEvent WITHIN 1 where
TargetInstance ISA 'Win32_Process'")


x=0
y=0

Function GetValue(ByVal Name, ByVal obj)
```

```
Dim tempstr, pos, pName
pName = Name
tempstr = obj.GetObjectText_
Name = Name + " = "
pos = InStr(tempstr, Name)
if pos Then
    pos = pos + Len(Name)
    tempstr = Mid(tempstr, pos, Len(tempstr))
    pos = InStr(tempstr, ";")
    tempstr = Mid(tempstr, 1, pos - 1)
    tempstr = Replace(tempstr, Chr(34), "")
    tempstr = Replace(tempstr, "{", "")
    tempstr = Replace(tempstr, "}", "")
    tempstr = Trim(tempstr)
    if len(tempstr) > 13 then
        if obj.Properties_(pName).CIMType = 101 Then
            tempstr = Mid(tempstr, 5, 2) + "/" + _
            Mid(tempstr, 7, 2) + "/" + _
            Mid(tempstr, 1, 4) + " " + _
            Mid(tempstr, 9, 2) + ":" + _
            Mid(tempstr, 11, 2) + ":" + _
            Mid(tempstr, 13, 2)
        End If
    End If
    GetValue = tempstr
Else
    GetValue = ""
End If

End Function


sub sink_OnObjectReady(objWbemObject, objWbemAsyncContext)
```

```
Set obj = objWbemObject.Properties_.Item("TargetInstance").Value

If y = 0 then
    For Each prop in obj.Properties_
        Call dNames.Add(x, prop.Name)
    Next
End if

Set dCols = CreateObject("Scripting.Dictionary")
For Each prop in obj.Properties_
    Call dCols.Add(x, GetValue(prop.Name, obj))
    x=x+1
Next
Call dRows.Add(y, dCols)
x = 0
y= y+1

End Sub

Sub              sink_OnCompleted(iHResult,              objWbemErrorObject,
objWbemAsyncContext)

    w = 1

End Sub

w = 0

Set l = CreateObject("WbemScripting.SWbemLocator")
Set svc = l.ConnectServer(".", "root\CIMV2")
svc.Security_.AuthenticationLevel = 6
```

```
svc.Security_.ImpersonationLevel = 3

Set mysink = WScript.CreateObject("WBemScripting.SWbemSink", "sink_")
Call svc.ExecNotificationQueryAsync(mysink, strQuery)

Do While w = 0
  WScript.Sleep(500)
Loop

Set ws = CreateObject("WScript.Shell")
Set fso = CreateObject("Scripting.FileSystemObject")
Set      txtstream      =      fso.OpenTextFile(ws.CurrentDirectory      +
"\Win32_Process.html", 2, true, -2)
txtstream.WriteLine("<html>")
txtstream.WriteLine("<head>")
txtstream.WriteLine("<style type='text/css'>")
txtstream.WriteLine("th")
txtstream.WriteLine("{")
txtstream.WriteLine("   COLOR: darkred;")
txtstream.WriteLine("   BACKGROUND-COLOR: white;")
txtstream.WriteLine("   FONT-FAMILY:font-family: Cambria, serif;")
txtstream.WriteLine("   FONT-SIZE: 12px;")
txtstream.WriteLine("   text-align: left;")
txtstream.WriteLine("   white-Space: nowrap;")
txtstream.WriteLine("}")
txtstream.WriteLine("td")
txtstream.WriteLine("{")
txtstream.WriteLine("   COLOR: navy;")
txtstream.WriteLine("   BACKGROUND-COLOR: white;")
txtstream.WriteLine("   FONT-FAMILY: font-family: Cambria, serif;")
txtstream.WriteLine("   FONT-SIZE: 12px;")
txtstream.WriteLine("   text-align: left;")
txtstream.WriteLine("   white-Space: nowrap;")
```

```
txtstream.WriteLine("}")
txtstream.WriteLine("</style>")
txtstream.WriteLine("<title>Win32_Process</title>")
txtstream.WriteLine("</head>")
txtstream.WriteLine("<body>")
txtstream.WriteLine("<table Border='1' cellpadding='1' cellspacing='1'>")
txtstream.WriteLine("<tr>")
Nkeys = dNames.Keys
for x = 0 To uBound(Nkeys) -1
    txtstream.WriteLine("<th>" & dNames(Nkeys(x)) & "</th>")
next
txtstream.WriteLine("</tr>")
Rkeys = dRows.Keys
for y = 0 to UBound(RKeys) -1
    txtstream.WriteLine("<tr>")
    Set DCols = dRows(RKeys(y))
    Ckeys = DCols.Keys
    for x = 0 To uBound(CKeys) -1
        txtstream.WriteLine("<td>" & DCols(CKeys(x)) & "</td>")
    next
    txtstream.WriteLine("</tr>")
next
txtstream.WriteLine("</table>")
txtstream.WriteLine("</body>")
txtstream.WriteLine("</html>")
txtstream.close
```

The many ways to use your WMI skills and impress people

The following is list of the what we're going to be using with WMI:

ASP

ASPX

Attribute XML

Delimited Files

Element XML

Element XML For XSL

Excel

HTA

HTML

Schema XML

XSL

I need to do this before someone complains.

Up to here, the various languages I'm going to cover will have the same chapters. But past here, the code is specifically for each language. All will have the same code examples but written in the language specified in the title.

Working with ASP

The concept of programs writing programs

NEED TO SHARE SOMETHING IMPOTANT WITH YOU THAT I HAVE SEEN ASKED BY PROS OVER AND OVER AGAIN. THE FACT THAT THEY ARE ASKING IT SHOWS JUST HOW UNAWARE THEY ARE OF THIS IMPORTANT FACT. Anything you write inside a textstream is considered by the compiler to be a string and not code.

So, if I type:

For VBScript, VB, VBS, VB.Net, Python, Ruby:

```
txtstream.WriteLine("Response.Write(""<tr>"" & vbcrlf) ")
```

For Javascript, JScript:

```
txtstream.WriteLine("Response.Write(""<tr>"" & vbcrlf) ");
```

For Kixtart:

```
$txtstream.WriteLine("Response.Write(""<tr>"" & vbcrlf) ")
```

For C#:

```
txtstream.WriteLine("Response.Write(\"<tr>\" & vbcrlf) ");
```

For C++:

```
txtstream->WriteLine("Response.Write(\"<tr>\" & vbcrlf) ");
```

For Perlscript:

```
$txtstream->WriteLine("Response.Write(""<tr>"" & vbcrlf) ");
```

For Rexx:

```
txtstream~WriteLine("Response.Write(""<tr>"" & vbcrlf) ")
```

For Borland C Builder:

txtstream.OLEFunction("WriteLine", OleVariant("Response.Write(""<tr>"" & vbcrlf) ");

For Borland Delphi:

txtstream.WriteLine('Response.Write("<tr> " & vbcrlf) ');

Aside from conforming to the compiler's expectations for single and double quotes, see any difference in the Response.Write("<tr>" & vbcrlf). It's because that part of the code is written to run as VBScript.

That also means any of the 14 languages listed could also create any of the other 14 languages. Hence, Programs that write programs. Below, is the code for ASP. The getValue function is in Appendix B.

```
y = 0
Set ws = CreateObject("WScript.Shell")
Set fso = CreateObject("Scripting.FileSystemObject")
Set        txtstream    =    fso.OpenTextFile(ws.CurrentDirectory    +
"\Win32_Process.asp", 2, true, -2)
```

For Single Line Horizontal

```
txtstream.WriteLine("<html>")
txtstream.WriteLine("<head>")
txtstream.WriteLine("<style type='text/css'>")
txtstream.WriteLine("th")
txtstream.WriteLine("{")
txtstream.WriteLine("    COLOR: darkred;")
txtstream.WriteLine("    BACKGROUND-COLOR: white;")
txtstream.WriteLine("    FONT-FAMILY:font-family: Cambria, serif;")
txtstream.WriteLine("    FONT-SIZE: 12px;")
txtstream.WriteLine("    text-align: left;")
txtstream.WriteLine("    white-Space: nowrap;")
txtstream.WriteLine("}")
```

```
txtstream.WriteLine("td")
txtstream.WriteLine("{")
txtstream.WriteLine("    COLOR: navy;")
txtstream.WriteLine("    BACKGROUND-COLOR: white;")
txtstream.WriteLine("    FONT-FAMILY: font-family: Cambria, serif;")
txtstream.WriteLine("    FONT-SIZE: 12px;")
txtstream.WriteLine("    text-align: left;")
txtstream.WriteLine("    white-Space: nowrap;")
txtstream.WriteLine("}")
txtstream.WriteLine("</style>")
txtstream.WriteLine("<title>Win32_Process</title>")
txtstream.WriteLine("</head>")
txtstream.WriteLine("<body>")
```

Use this if you want to create a border around your table:
```
txtstream.WriteLine("<table Border='1' cellpadding='1' cellspacing='1'>")
```

Use this if you don't want to create a border around your table:
```
txtstream.WriteLine("<table Border='0' cellpadding='1' cellspacing='1'>")
```

```
txtstream.WriteLine("<%")
```

```
txtstream.WriteLine("Response.Write(""<tr>"" & vbcrlf)")
for x = 0 to UBound(Names)-1
    txtstream.WriteLine("Response.Write(""<th>" & prop.Name & "</th>"" & vbcrlf)")
next
txtstream.WriteLine("Response.Write(""</tr>"" & vbcrlf)")
txtstream.WriteLine("Response.Write(""<tr>"" & vbcrlf)")
```

```
for x = 0 to UBound(Names)-1
   C = Rows(0)
   txtstream.WriteLine("Response.Write(""<td>" & C(x) & "</td>""" & vbcrlf)")
next
txtstream.WriteLine("Response.Write(""</tr>""" & vbcrlf)")
txtstream.WriteLine("%>")
txtstream.WriteLine("</table>")
txtstream.WriteLine("</body>")
txtstream.WriteLine("</html>")
txtstream.close
```

For Multi Line Horizontal

```
txtstream.WriteLine("<html>")
txtstream.WriteLine("<head>")
txtstream.WriteLine("<style type='text/css'>")
txtstream.WriteLine("th")
txtstream.WriteLine("{")
txtstream.WriteLine("   COLOR: darkred;")
txtstream.WriteLine("   BACKGROUND-COLOR: white;")
txtstream.WriteLine("   FONT-FAMILY:font-family: Cambria, serif;")
txtstream.WriteLine("   FONT-SIZE: 12px;")
txtstream.WriteLine("   text-align: left;")
txtstream.WriteLine("   white-Space: nowrap;")
txtstream.WriteLine("}")
txtstream.WriteLine("td")
txtstream.WriteLine("{")
txtstream.WriteLine("   COLOR: navy;")
txtstream.WriteLine("   BACKGROUND-COLOR: white;")
txtstream.WriteLine("   FONT-FAMILY: font-family: Cambria, serif;")
txtstream.WriteLine("   FONT-SIZE: 12px;")
```

```
txtstream.WriteLine("    text-align: left;")
txtstream.WriteLine("    white-Space: nowrap;")
txtstream.WriteLine("}")
txtstream.WriteLine("</style>")
txtstream.WriteLine("<title>Win32_Process</title>")
txtstream.WriteLine("</head>")
txtstream.WriteLine("<body>")
```

Use this if you want to create a border around your table:
```
txtstream.WriteLine("<table Border='1' cellpadding='1' cellspacing='1'>")
```

Use this if you don't want to create a border around your table:
```
txtstream.WriteLine("<table Border='0' cellpadding='1' cellspacing='1'>")
```

```
txtstream.WriteLine("<%")

txtstream.WriteLine("Response.Write(""<tr>"" & vbcrlf)")
for x = 0 to UBound(Names)-1
    txtstream.WriteLine("Response.Write(""<th>" & Names(x) & "</th>"" & vbcrlf)")
next
txtstream.WriteLine("Response.Write(""</tr>"" & vbcrlf)")
for y = 0 to ubound(Values) -1
    C = Rows(y)
    txtstream.WriteLine("Response.Write(""<tr>"" & vbcrlf)")
    for x = 0 to UBound(Names)-1
        txtstream.WriteLine("Response.Write(""<td>" & C(x) & "</td>"" & vbcrlf)")
    next
    txtstream.WriteLine("Response.Write(""</tr>"" & vbcrlf)")
Next
txtstream.WriteLine("%>")
txtstream.WriteLine("</table>")
```

```
txtstream.WriteLine("</body>")
txtstream.WriteLine("</html>")
txtstream.close
```

For Single Line Vertical

```
txtstream.WriteLine("<html>")
txtstream.WriteLine("<head>")
txtstream.WriteLine("<style type='text/css'>")
txtstream.WriteLine("th")
txtstream.WriteLine("{")
txtstream.WriteLine("   COLOR: darkred;")
txtstream.WriteLine("   BACKGROUND-COLOR: white;")
txtstream.WriteLine("   FONT-FAMILY:font-family: Cambria, serif;")
txtstream.WriteLine("   FONT-SIZE: 12px;")
txtstream.WriteLine("   text-align: left;")
txtstream.WriteLine("   white-Space: nowrap;")
txtstream.WriteLine("}")
txtstream.WriteLine("td")
txtstream.WriteLine("{")
txtstream.WriteLine("   COLOR: navy;")
txtstream.WriteLine("   BACKGROUND-COLOR: white;")
txtstream.WriteLine("   FONT-FAMILY: font-family: Cambria, serif;")
txtstream.WriteLine("   FONT-SIZE: 12px;")
txtstream.WriteLine("   text-align: left;")
txtstream.WriteLine("   white-Space: nowrap;")
txtstream.WriteLine("}")
txtstream.WriteLine("</style>")
txtstream.WriteLine("<title>Win32_Process</title>")
txtstream.WriteLine("</head>")
txtstream.WriteLine("<body>")
```

Use this if you want to create a border around your table:
```
txtstream.WriteLine("<table Border='1' cellpadding='1' cellspacing='1'>")
```

Use this if you don't want to create a border around your table:

```
txtstream.WriteLine("<table Border='0' cellpadding='1' cellspacing='1'>")

txtstream.WriteLine("<%")
C = Rows(0)
for x = 0 to UBound(Names)-1
    txtstream.WriteLine("Response.Write(""<tr><th>"    &    Names(x)    &
"</th><td>" & C(x) & "</td></tr>"" & vbcrlf)")
    next
txtstream.WriteLine("%>")
txtstream.WriteLine("</table>")
txtstream.WriteLine("</body>")
txtstream.WriteLine("</html>")
txtstream.close
```

For Multi Line Vertical

```
txtstream.WriteLine("<html>")
txtstream.WriteLine("<head>")
txtstream.WriteLine("<style type='text/css'>")
txtstream.WriteLine("th")
txtstream.WriteLine("{")
txtstream.WriteLine("    COLOR: darkred;")
txtstream.WriteLine("    BACKGROUND-COLOR: white;")
txtstream.WriteLine("    FONT-FAMILY:font-family: Cambria, serif;")
txtstream.WriteLine("    FONT-SIZE: 12px;")
txtstream.WriteLine("    text-align: left;")
txtstream.WriteLine("    white-Space: nowrap;")
txtstream.WriteLine("}")
txtstream.WriteLine("td")
txtstream.WriteLine("{")
txtstream.WriteLine("    COLOR: navy;")
```

```
txtstream.WriteLine("    BACKGROUND-COLOR: white;")
txtstream.WriteLine("    FONT-FAMILY: font-family: Cambria, serif;")
txtstream.WriteLine("    FONT-SIZE: 12px;")
txtstream.WriteLine("    text-align: left;")
txtstream.WriteLine("    white-Space: nowrap;")
txtstream.WriteLine("}")
txtstream.WriteLine("</style>")
txtstream.WriteLine("<title>Win32_Process</title>")
txtstream.WriteLine("</head>")
txtstream.WriteLine("<body>")
```

Use this if you want to create a border around your table:
```
txtstream.WriteLine("<table Border='1' cellpadding='1' cellspacing='1'>")
```

Use this if you don't want to create a border around your table:
```
txtstream.WriteLine("<table Border='0' cellpadding='1' cellspacing='1'>")
txtstream.WriteLine("<%")
```

```
for x = 0 to UBound(Names)-1
    txtstream.WriteLine("Response.Write(""<tr><th>" & Names(x) & "</th>""
& vbcrlf)")
        for y = 0 to ubound(Values) -1
        C = Rows(y)
        txtstream.WriteLine("Response.Write(""<td>" & C(x) & "</td>"" &
vbcrlf)")
    next
    txtstream.WriteLine("Response.Write(""</tr>"" & vbcrlf)")
Next
txtstream.WriteLine("%>")
txtstream.WriteLine("</table>")
txtstream.WriteLine("</body>")
txtstream.WriteLine("</html>")
txtstream.close
```

ASPX Code

B elow, is the code for ASP. The getValue function is in Appendix B.

```
Set ws = CreateObject("WScript.Shell")
Set fso = CreateObject("Scripting.FileSystemObject")
Set    txtstream    =    fso.OpenTextFile(ws.CurrentDirectory    +
"\Win32_Process.aspx", 2, true, -2)
y = 0
```

For Single Line Horizontal

```
txtstream.WriteLine("<!DOCTYPE html PUBLIC ""-//W3C//DTD XHTML 1.0
Transitional//EN"" ""http://www.w3.org/TR/xhtml1/DTD/xhtml1-
transitional.dtd"">")
txtstream.WriteLine("")
txtstream.WriteLine("<html xmlns="http://www.w3.org/1999/xhtml"
>")
txtstream.WriteLine("<head>")
txtstream.WriteLine("<style type='text/css'>")
txtstream.WriteLine("th")
txtstream.WriteLine("{")
txtstream.WriteLine("    COLOR: darkred;")
```

```
txtstream.WriteLine("    BACKGROUND-COLOR: white;")
txtstream.WriteLine("    FONT-FAMILY:font-family: Cambria, serif;")
txtstream.WriteLine("    FONT-SIZE: 12px;")
txtstream.WriteLine("    text-align: left;")
txtstream.WriteLine("    white-Space: nowrap;")
txtstream.WriteLine("}")
txtstream.WriteLine("td")
txtstream.WriteLine("{")
txtstream.WriteLine("    COLOR: navy;")
txtstream.WriteLine("    BACKGROUND-COLOR: white;")
txtstream.WriteLine("    FONT-FAMILY: font-family: Cambria, serif;")
txtstream.WriteLine("    FONT-SIZE: 12px;")
txtstream.WriteLine("    text-align: left;")
txtstream.WriteLine("    white-Space: nowrap;")
txtstream.WriteLine("}")
txtstream.WriteLine("</style>")
txtstream.WriteLine("<title>Win32_Process</title>")
txtstream.WriteLine("</head>")
txtstream.WriteLine("<body>")
```

Use this if you want to create a border around your table:
```
txtstream.WriteLine("<table Border='1' cellpadding='1' cellspacing='1'>")
```

Use this if you don't want to create a border around your table:
```
txtstream.WriteLine("<table Border='0' cellpadding='1' cellspacing='1'>")
txtstream.WriteLine("<%")
```

```
txtstream.WriteLine("Response.Write(""<tr>"" & vbcrlf)")
for x = 0 to UBound(Names)-1
    txtstream.WriteLine("Response.Write(""<th>" & Names(x) & "</th>"" & vbcrlf)")
next
txtstream.WriteLine("Response.Write(""</tr>"" & vbcrlf)")
```

```
txtstream.WriteLine("Response.Write("""<tr>""" & vbcrlf)")
C = Rows(0)
for x = 0 to UBound(Names)-1
    txtstream.WriteLine("Response.Write("""<td>" & C(x) & "</td>""" & vbcrlf)")
next
txtstream.WriteLine("Response.Write("""</tr>""" & vbcrlf)")
txtstream.WriteLine("%>")
txtstream.WriteLine("</table>")
txtstream.WriteLine("</body>")
txtstream.WriteLine("</html>")
txtstream.close
```

For Multi Line Horizontal

```
txtstream.WriteLine("<!DOCTYPE html PUBLIC ""-//W3C//DTD XHTML 1.0
Transitional//EN"" ""http://www.w3.org/TR/xhtml1/DTD/xhtml1-
transitional.dtd"">")
txtstream.WriteLine("")
txtstream.WriteLine("<html xmlns="http://www.w3.org/1999/xhtml"
>")
txtstream.WriteLine("<head>")
txtstream.WriteLine("<style type='text/css'>")
txtstream.WriteLine("th")
txtstream.WriteLine("{")
txtstream.WriteLine("   COLOR: darkred;")
txtstream.WriteLine("   BACKGROUND-COLOR: white;")
txtstream.WriteLine("   FONT-FAMILY:font-family: Cambria, serif;")
txtstream.WriteLine("   FONT-SIZE: 12px;")
txtstream.WriteLine("   text-align: left;")
txtstream.WriteLine("   white-Space: nowrap;")
txtstream.WriteLine("}")
txtstream.WriteLine("td")
txtstream.WriteLine("{")
txtstream.WriteLine("   COLOR: navy;")
```

```vbscript
txtstream.WriteLine("    BACKGROUND-COLOR: white;")
txtstream.WriteLine("    FONT-FAMILY: font-family: Cambria, serif;")
txtstream.WriteLine("    FONT-SIZE: 12px;")
txtstream.WriteLine("    text-align: left;")
txtstream.WriteLine("    white-Space: nowrap;")
txtstream.WriteLine("}")
txtstream.WriteLine("</style>")
txtstream.WriteLine("<title>Win32_Process</title>")
txtstream.WriteLine("</head>")
txtstream.WriteLine("<body>")
```

Use this if you want to create a border around your table:

```vbscript
txtstream.WriteLine("<table Border='1' cellpadding='1' cellspacing='1'>")
```

Use this if you don't want to create a border around your table:

```vbscript
txtstream.WriteLine("<table Border='0' cellpadding='1' cellspacing='1'>")

txtstream.WriteLine("<%")

txtstream.WriteLine("Response.Write(""<tr>"" & vbcrlf)")
for x = 0 to UBound(Names)-1
    txtstream.WriteLine("Response.Write(""<th>" & Names(x) & "</th>"" & vbcrlf)")
next
txtstream.WriteLine("Response.Write(""</tr>"" & vbcrlf)")
for y = 0 to ubound(Values) -1
    C = Rows(y)
    txtstream.WriteLine("Response.Write(""<tr>"" & vbcrlf)")
    for x = 0 to UBound(Names)-1
        txtstream.WriteLine("Response.Write(""<td>" & C(x) & "</td>"" & vbcrlf)")
    next
    txtstream.WriteLine("Response.Write(""</tr>"" & vbcrlf)")
```

Next

txtstream.WriteLine("%>")

txtstream.WriteLine("</table>")

txtstream.WriteLine("</body>")

txtstream.WriteLine("</html>")

txtstream.close

For Single Line Vertical

txtstream.WriteLine("<!DOCTYPE html PUBLIC ""-//W3C//DTD XHTML 1.0 Transitional//EN"" ""http://www.w3.org/TR/xhtml1/DTD/xhtml1-transitional.dtd"">")

txtstream.WriteLine("")

txtstream.WriteLine("<html xmlns="http://www.w3.org/1999/xhtml">")

txtstream.WriteLine("<head>")

txtstream.WriteLine("<style type='text/css'>")

txtstream.WriteLine("th")

txtstream.WriteLine("{")

txtstream.WriteLine("   COLOR: darkred;")

txtstream.WriteLine("   BACKGROUND-COLOR: white;")

txtstream.WriteLine("   FONT-FAMILY:font-family: Cambria, serif;")

txtstream.WriteLine("   FONT-SIZE: 12px;")

txtstream.WriteLine("   text-align: left;")

txtstream.WriteLine("   white-Space: nowrap;")

txtstream.WriteLine("}")

txtstream.WriteLine("td")

txtstream.WriteLine("{")

txtstream.WriteLine("   COLOR: navy;")

txtstream.WriteLine("   BACKGROUND-COLOR: white;")

txtstream.WriteLine("   FONT-FAMILY: font-family: Cambria, serif;")

txtstream.WriteLine("   FONT-SIZE: 12px;")

txtstream.WriteLine("   text-align: left;")

txtstream.WriteLine("   white-Space: nowrap;")

txtstream.WriteLine("}")

```
txtstream.WriteLine("</style>")
txtstream.WriteLine("<title>Win32_Process</title>")
txtstream.WriteLine("</head>")
txtstream.WriteLine("<body>")
```

Use this if you want to create a border around your table:
```
txtstream.WriteLine("<table Border='1' cellpadding='1' cellspacing='1'>")
```

Use this if you don't want to create a border around your table:
```
txtstream.WriteLine("<table Border='0' cellpadding='1' cellspacing='1'>")
```

```
txtstream.WriteLine("<%")
C = Rows(0)
for x = 0 to UBound(Names)-1
    txtstream.WriteLine("Response.Write(""<tr><th>"        &        Names(x)        &
"</th><td>" & C(x) & "</td></tr>"" & vbcrlf)")
next
txtstream.WriteLine("%>")
txtstream.WriteLine("</table>")
txtstream.WriteLine("</body>")
txtstream.WriteLine("</html>")
txtstream.close
```

For Multi Line Vertical

```
txtstream.WriteLine("<!DOCTYPE html PUBLIC ""-//W3C//DTD XHTML 1.0
Transitional//EN"" ""http://www.w3.org/TR/xhtml1/DTD/xhtml1-
transitional.dtd"">")
txtstream.WriteLine("")
txtstream.WriteLine("<html xmlns="http://www.w3.org/1999/xhtml"
>")
txtstream.WriteLine("<head>")
txtstream.WriteLine("<style type='text/css'>")
txtstream.WriteLine("th")
```

```
txtstream.WriteLine("{")
txtstream.WriteLine("   COLOR: darkred;")
txtstream.WriteLine("   BACKGROUND-COLOR: white;")
txtstream.WriteLine("   FONT-FAMILY:font-family: Cambria, serif;")
txtstream.WriteLine("   FONT-SIZE: 12px;")
txtstream.WriteLine("   text-align: left;")
txtstream.WriteLine("   white-Space: nowrap;")
txtstream.WriteLine("}")
txtstream.WriteLine("td")
txtstream.WriteLine("{")
txtstream.WriteLine("   COLOR: navy;")
txtstream.WriteLine("   BACKGROUND-COLOR: white;")
txtstream.WriteLine("   FONT-FAMILY: font-family: Cambria, serif;")
txtstream.WriteLine("   FONT-SIZE: 12px;")
txtstream.WriteLine("   text-align: left;")
txtstream.WriteLine("   white-Space: nowrap;")
txtstream.WriteLine("}")
txtstream.WriteLine("</style>")
txtstream.WriteLine("<title>Win32_Process</title>")
txtstream.WriteLine("</head>")
txtstream.WriteLine("<body>")
```

Use this if you want to create a border around your table:
```
txtstream.WriteLine("<table Border='1' cellpadding='1' cellspacing='1'>")
```

Use this if you don't want to create a border around your table:
```
txtstream.WriteLine("<table Border='0' cellpadding='1' cellspacing='1'>")
```

```
txtstream.WriteLine("<%")
```

```
for x = 0 to UBound(Names)-1
    txtstream.WriteLine("Response.Write(""<tr><th>" & Names(x) & "</th>"""
& vbcrlf)")
```

```
    for y = 0 to ubound(Values) -1
      C = Rows(y)
      txtstream.WriteLine("Response.Write(""<td>"  &  C(x)  &  "</td>"""  &
vbcrlf)")
    next
    txtstream.WriteLine("Response.Write(""</tr>""" & vbcrlf)")
  Next
  txtstream.WriteLine("%>")
  txtstream.WriteLine("</table>")
  txtstream.WriteLine("</body>")
  txtstream.WriteLine("</html>")
  txtstream.close
```

HTA Code

B elow, is the code for HTA. The getValue function is in Appendix B.

```
Set ws = CreateObject("WScript.Shell")
Set fso = CreateObject("Scripting.FileSystemObject")
Set txtstream = fso.OpenTextFile(ws.CurrentDirectory + "\Win32_Process.hta",
2, true, -2)
    y=0
```

For Single Line Horizontal

```
txtstream.WriteLine("<html>")
txtstream.WriteLine("<head>")
txtstream.WriteLine("<HTA:APPLICATION ")
txtstream.WriteLine("ID = ""Process"" ")
txtstream.WriteLine("APPLICATIONNAME = ""Process"" ")
txtstream.WriteLine("SCROLL = ""yes"" ")
txtstream.WriteLine("SINGLEINSTANCE = ""yes"" ")
txtstream.WriteLine("WINDOWSTATE = ""maximize"" >")
txtstream.WriteLine("<style type='text/css'>")
```

```
txtstream.WriteLine("th")
txtstream.WriteLine("{")
txtstream.WriteLine("   COLOR: darkred;")
txtstream.WriteLine("   BACKGROUND-COLOR: white;")
txtstream.WriteLine("   FONT-FAMILY:font-family: Cambria, serif;")
txtstream.WriteLine("   FONT-SIZE: 12px;")
txtstream.WriteLine("   text-align: left;")
txtstream.WriteLine("   white-Space: nowrap;")
txtstream.WriteLine("}")
txtstream.WriteLine("td")
txtstream.WriteLine("{")
txtstream.WriteLine("   COLOR: navy;")
txtstream.WriteLine("   BACKGROUND-COLOR: white;")
txtstream.WriteLine("   FONT-FAMILY: font-family: Cambria, serif;")
txtstream.WriteLine("   FONT-SIZE: 12px;")
txtstream.WriteLine("   text-align: left;")
txtstream.WriteLine("   white-Space: nowrap;")
txtstream.WriteLine("}")
txtstream.WriteLine("</style>")
txtstream.WriteLine("<title>Win32_Process</title>")
txtstream.WriteLine("</head>")
txtstream.WriteLine("<body>")
```

Use this if you want to create a border around your table:
```
txtstream.WriteLine("<table Border='1' cellpadding='1' cellspacing='1'>")
```

Use this if you don't want to create a border around your table:
```
txtstream.WriteLine("<table Border='0' cellpadding='1' cellspacing='1'>")
```

```
txtstream.WriteLine("<tr>")
for x = 0 to UBound(Names)-1
    txtstream.WriteLine("<th>" & Names(x) & "</th>")
next
```

```
txtstream.WriteLine("</tr>")
txtstream.WriteLine("<tr>")
C = Rows(0)
for x = 0 to UBound(Names)-1
    txtstream.WriteLine("<td>" & C(x) & "</td>")
next
txtstream.WriteLine("</tr>")
txtstream.WriteLine("</table>")
txtstream.WriteLine("</body>")
txtstream.WriteLine("</html>")
txtstream.close
```

For Multi Line Horizontal

```
txtstream.WriteLine(html>")
txtstream.WriteLine("<head>")
txtstream.WriteLine("<HTA:APPLICATION ")
txtstream.WriteLine("ID = ""Process"" ")
txtstream.WriteLine("APPLICATIONNAME = ""Process"" ")
txtstream.WriteLine("SCROLL = ""yes"" ")
txtstream.WriteLine("SINGLEINSTANCE = ""yes"" ")
txtstream.WriteLine("WINDOWSTATE = ""maximize"" >")
txtstream.WriteLine("<style type='text/css'>")
txtstream.WriteLine("th")
txtstream.WriteLine("{")
txtstream.WriteLine("    COLOR: darkred;")
txtstream.WriteLine("    BACKGROUND-COLOR: white;")
txtstream.WriteLine("    FONT-FAMILY:font-family: Cambria, serif;")
txtstream.WriteLine("    FONT-SIZE: 12px;")
txtstream.WriteLine("    text-align: left;")
txtstream.WriteLine("    white-Space: nowrap;")
txtstream.WriteLine("}")
txtstream.WriteLine("td")
```

```
txtstream.WriteLine("{")
txtstream.WriteLine("    COLOR: navy;")
txtstream.WriteLine("    BACKGROUND-COLOR: white;")
txtstream.WriteLine("    FONT-FAMILY: font-family: Cambria, serif;")
txtstream.WriteLine("    FONT-SIZE: 12px;")
txtstream.WriteLine("    text-align: left;")
txtstream.WriteLine("    white-Space: nowrap;")
txtstream.WriteLine("}")
txtstream.WriteLine("</style>")
txtstream.WriteLine("<title>Win32_Process</title>")
txtstream.WriteLine("</head>")
txtstream.WriteLine("<body>")
```

Use this if you want to create a border around your table:
```
txtstream.WriteLine("<table Border='1' cellpadding='1' cellspacing='1'>")
```

Use this if you don't want to create a border around your table:
```
txtstream.WriteLine("<table Border='0' cellpadding='1' cellspacing='1'>")
```

```
txtstream.WriteLine("<tr>")
for x = 0 to UBound(Names)-1
    txtstream.WriteLine("<th>" & Names(x) & "</th>")
next
txtstream.WriteLine("</tr>")
for y = 0 to ubound(Values) -1
    C = Rows(y)
    txtstream.WriteLine("<tr>")
    for x = 0 to UBound(Names)-1
        txtstream.WriteLine("<td>" & C(x) & "</td>")
    next
    txtstream.WriteLine("</tr>")
Next
```

```
txtstream.WriteLine("</table>")
txtstream.WriteLine("</body>")
txtstream.WriteLine("</html>")
txtstream.close
```

For Single Line Vertical

```
txtstream.WriteLine("<html>")
txtstream.WriteLine("<head>")
txtstream.WriteLine("<HTA:APPLICATION ")
txtstream.WriteLine("ID = """Process""" ")
txtstream.WriteLine("APPLICATIONNAME = """Process""" ")
txtstream.WriteLine("SCROLL = """yes""" ")
txtstream.WriteLine("SINGLEINSTANCE = """yes""" ")
txtstream.WriteLine("WINDOWSTATE = """maximize""" >")

txtstream.WriteLine("<style type='text/css'>")
txtstream.WriteLine("th")
txtstream.WriteLine("{")
txtstream.WriteLine("    COLOR: darkred;")
txtstream.WriteLine("    BACKGROUND-COLOR: white;")
txtstream.WriteLine("    FONT-FAMILY:font-family: Cambria, serif;")
txtstream.WriteLine("    FONT-SIZE: 12px;")
txtstream.WriteLine("    text-align: left;")
txtstream.WriteLine("    white-Space: nowrap;")
txtstream.WriteLine("}")
txtstream.WriteLine("td")
txtstream.WriteLine("{")
txtstream.WriteLine("    COLOR: navy;")
txtstream.WriteLine("    BACKGROUND-COLOR: white;")
txtstream.WriteLine("    FONT-FAMILY: font-family: Cambria, serif;")
txtstream.WriteLine("    FONT-SIZE: 12px;")
```

```
txtstream.WriteLine("    text-align: left;")
txtstream.WriteLine("    white-Space: nowrap;")
txtstream.WriteLine("}")
txtstream.WriteLine("</style>")
txtstream.WriteLine("<title>Win32_Process</title>")
txtstream.WriteLine("</head>")
txtstream.WriteLine("<body>")
```

Use this if you want to create a border around your table:

```
txtstream.WriteLine("<table Border='1' cellpadding='1' cellspacing='1'>")
```

Use this if you don't want to create a border around your table:

```
txtstream.WriteLine("<table Border='0' cellpadding='1' cellspacing='1'>")
C = Rows(0)
for x = 0 to UBound(Names)-1
    txtstream.WriteLine("<tr><th>" & Names(x) & "</th><td>" & C(x) &
"</td></tr>")
    next
txtstream.WriteLine("</table>")
txtstream.WriteLine("</body>")
txtstream.WriteLine("</html>")
txtstream.close
```

For Multi Line Vertical

```
txtstream.WriteLine("<html>")
txtstream.WriteLine("<head>")
txtstream.WriteLine("<HTA:APPLICATION ")
txtstream.WriteLine("ID = ""Process"" ")
txtstream.WriteLine("APPLICATIONNAME = ""Process"" ")
txtstream.WriteLine("SCROLL = ""yes"" ")
txtstream.WriteLine("SINGLEINSTANCE = ""yes"" ")
txtstream.WriteLine("WINDOWSTATE = ""maximize"" >")
```

```
txtstream.WriteLine("<style type='text/css'>")
txtstream.WriteLine("th")
txtstream.WriteLine("{")
txtstream.WriteLine("    COLOR: darkred;")
txtstream.WriteLine("    BACKGROUND-COLOR: white;")
txtstream.WriteLine("    FONT-FAMILY:font-family: Cambria, serif;")
txtstream.WriteLine("    FONT-SIZE: 12px;")
txtstream.WriteLine("    text-align: left;")
txtstream.WriteLine("    white-Space: nowrap;")
txtstream.WriteLine("}")
txtstream.WriteLine("td")
txtstream.WriteLine("{")
txtstream.WriteLine("    COLOR: navy;")
txtstream.WriteLine("    BACKGROUND-COLOR: white;")
txtstream.WriteLine("    FONT-FAMILY: font-family: Cambria, serif;")
txtstream.WriteLine("    FONT-SIZE: 12px;")
txtstream.WriteLine("    text-align: left;")
txtstream.WriteLine("    white-Space: nowrap;")
txtstream.WriteLine("}")
txtstream.WriteLine("</style>")
txtstream.WriteLine("<title>Win32_Process</title>")
txtstream.WriteLine("</head>")
txtstream.WriteLine("<body>")
```

Use this if you want to create a border around your table:
```
txtstream.WriteLine("<table Border='1' cellpadding='1' cellspacing='1'>")
```

Use this if you don't want to create a border around your table:
```
txtstream.WriteLine("<table Border='0' cellpadding='1' cellspacing='1'>")
```

```
for x = 0 to UBound(Names)-1
   txtstream.WriteLine("<tr><th>" & Names(x) & "</th>")
   for y = 0 to ubound(Values) -1
```

```
        C= Rows(y)
        txtstream.WriteLine("<td>" & C(x) & "</td>")
      next
      txtstream.WriteLine("</tr>")
Next
txtstream.WriteLine("</table>")
txtstream.WriteLine("</body>")
txtstream.WriteLine("</html>")
txtstream.close
```

HTML Code

Below, is the code for HTML. The getValue function is in Appendix B.

```
Set ws = CreateObject("WScript.Shell")
Set fso = CreateObject("Scripting.FileSystemObject")
Set    txtstream    =    fso.OpenTextFile(ws.CurrentDirectory    +
"\Win32_Process.html", 2, true, -2)
```

For Single Line Horizontal

```
txtstream.WriteLine("<html>")
txtstream.WriteLine("<head>")
txtstream.WriteLine("<style type='text/css'>")
txtstream.WriteLine("th")
txtstream.WriteLine("{")
txtstream.WriteLine("    COLOR: darkred;")
txtstream.WriteLine("    BACKGROUND-COLOR: white;")
txtstream.WriteLine("    FONT-FAMILY:font-family: Cambria, serif;")
txtstream.WriteLine("    FONT-SIZE: 12px;")
txtstream.WriteLine("    text-align: left;")
```

```
txtstream.WriteLine("    white-Space: nowrap;")
txtstream.WriteLine("}")
txtstream.WriteLine("td")
txtstream.WriteLine("{")
txtstream.WriteLine("    COLOR: navy;")
txtstream.WriteLine("    BACKGROUND-COLOR: white;")
txtstream.WriteLine("    FONT-FAMILY: font-family: Cambria, serif;")
txtstream.WriteLine("    FONT-SIZE: 12px;")
txtstream.WriteLine("    text-align: left;")
txtstream.WriteLine("    white-Space: nowrap;")
txtstream.WriteLine("}")
txtstream.WriteLine("</style>")
txtstream.WriteLine("<title>Win32_Process</title>")
txtstream.WriteLine("</head>")
txtstream.WriteLine("<body>")
```

Use this if you want to create a border around your table:
```
txtstream.WriteLine("<table Border='1' cellpadding='1' cellspacing='1'>")
```

Use this if you don't want to create a border around your table:
```
txtstream.WriteLine("<table Border='0' cellpadding='1' cellspacing='1'>")
```

```
txtstream.WriteLine("<tr>")
for x = 0 to UBound(Names)-1
    txtstream.WriteLine("<th>" & Names(x) & "</th>")
next
txtstream.WriteLine("</tr>")
txtstream.WriteLine("<tr>")
C = Rows(y)
for x = 0 to UBound(Names)-1
    txtstream.WriteLine("<td>" & C(x) & "</td>")
next
txtstream.WriteLine("</tr>")
```

```
txtstream.WriteLine("</table>")
txtstream.WriteLine("</body>")
txtstream.WriteLine("</html>")
txtstream.close
```

For Multi Line Horizontal

```
txtstream.WriteLine(html>")
txtstream.WriteLine("<head>")
txtstream.WriteLine("<style type='text/css'>")
txtstream.WriteLine("th")
txtstream.WriteLine("{")
txtstream.WriteLine("   COLOR: darkred;")
txtstream.WriteLine("   BACKGROUND-COLOR: white;")
txtstream.WriteLine("   FONT-FAMILY:font-family: Cambria, serif;")
txtstream.WriteLine("   FONT-SIZE: 12px;")
txtstream.WriteLine("    text-align: left;")
txtstream.WriteLine("   white-Space: nowrap;")
txtstream.WriteLine("}")
txtstream.WriteLine("td")
txtstream.WriteLine("{")
txtstream.WriteLine("   COLOR: navy;")
txtstream.WriteLine("   BACKGROUND-COLOR: white;")
txtstream.WriteLine("   FONT-FAMILY: font-family: Cambria, serif;")
txtstream.WriteLine("   FONT-SIZE: 12px;")
txtstream.WriteLine("    text-align: left;")
txtstream.WriteLine("   white-Space: nowrap;")
txtstream.WriteLine("}")
txtstream.WriteLine("</style>")
txtstream.WriteLine("<title>Win32_Process</title>")
txtstream.WriteLine("</head>")
txtstream.WriteLine("<body>")
```

Use this if you want to create a border around your table:
txtstream.WriteLine("<table Border='1' cellpadding='1' cellspacing='1'>")

Use this if you don't want to create a border around your table:
txtstream.WriteLine("<table Border='0' cellpadding='1' cellspacing='1'>")


```
txtstream.WriteLine("<tr>")
for x = 0 to UBound(Names)-1
   txtstream.WriteLine("<th>" & Names(x) & "</th>")
next
txtstream.WriteLine("</tr>")
for y = 0 to ubound(Values) -1
  C = Rows(y)
  txtstream.WriteLine("<tr>")
  for x = 0 to UBound(Names)-1
     txtstream.WriteLine("<td>" & C(x) & "</td>")
  next
  txtstream.WriteLine("</tr>")
Next
txtstream.WriteLine("</table>")
txtstream.WriteLine("</body>")
txtstream.WriteLine("</html>")
txtstream.close
```


For Single Line Vertical

```
txtstream.WriteLine("<html>")
txtstream.WriteLine("<head>")
txtstream.WriteLine("<style type='text/css'>")
txtstream.WriteLine("th")
txtstream.WriteLine("{")
```

```
txtstream.WriteLine("   COLOR: darkred;")
txtstream.WriteLine("   BACKGROUND-COLOR: white;")
txtstream.WriteLine("   FONT-FAMILY:font-family: Cambria, serif;")
txtstream.WriteLine("   FONT-SIZE: 12px;")
txtstream.WriteLine("   text-align: left;")
txtstream.WriteLine("   white-Space: nowrap;")
txtstream.WriteLine("}")
txtstream.WriteLine("td")
txtstream.WriteLine("{")
txtstream.WriteLine("   COLOR: navy;")
txtstream.WriteLine("   BACKGROUND-COLOR: white;")
txtstream.WriteLine("   FONT-FAMILY: font-family: Cambria, serif;")
txtstream.WriteLine("   FONT-SIZE: 12px;")
txtstream.WriteLine("   text-align: left;")
txtstream.WriteLine("   white-Space: nowrap;")
txtstream.WriteLine("}")
txtstream.WriteLine("</style>")
txtstream.WriteLine("<title>Win32_Process</title>")
txtstream.WriteLine("</head>")
txtstream.WriteLine("<body>")
```

Use this if you want to create a border around your table:
```
txtstream.WriteLine("<table Border='1' cellpadding='1' cellspacing='1'>")
```

Use this if you don't want to create a border around your table:
```
txtstream.WriteLine("<table Border='0' cellpadding='1' cellspacing='1'>")
```

```
C = Rows(0)
for x = 0 to UBound(Names)-1
    txtstream.WriteLine("<tr><th>" & Names(x) & "</th><td>" & C(x) &
"</td></tr>")
    next
    txtstream.WriteLine("</table>")
```

```
txtstream.WriteLine("</body>")
txtstream.WriteLine("</html>")
txtstream.close
```

For Multi Line Vertical

```
txtstream.WriteLine("<html>")
txtstream.WriteLine("<head>")
txtstream.WriteLine("<style type='text/css'>")
txtstream.WriteLine("th")
txtstream.WriteLine("{")
txtstream.WriteLine("   COLOR: darkred;")
txtstream.WriteLine("   BACKGROUND-COLOR: white;")
txtstream.WriteLine("   FONT-FAMILY:font-family: Cambria, serif;")
txtstream.WriteLine("   FONT-SIZE: 12px;")
txtstream.WriteLine("   text-align: left;")
txtstream.WriteLine("   white-Space: nowrap;")
txtstream.WriteLine("}")
txtstream.WriteLine("td")
txtstream.WriteLine("{")
txtstream.WriteLine("   COLOR: navy;")
txtstream.WriteLine("   BACKGROUND-COLOR: white;")
txtstream.WriteLine("   FONT-FAMILY: font-family: Cambria, serif;")
txtstream.WriteLine("   FONT-SIZE: 12px;")
txtstream.WriteLine("   text-align: left;")
txtstream.WriteLine("   white-Space: nowrap;")
txtstream.WriteLine("}")
txtstream.WriteLine("</style>")
txtstream.WriteLine("<title>Win32_Process</title>")
txtstream.WriteLine("</head>")
txtstream.WriteLine("<body>")
```

Use this if you want to create a border around your table:
```
txtstream.WriteLine("<table Border='1' cellpadding='1' cellspacing='1'>")
```

Use this if you don't want to create a border around your table:

```
txtstream.WriteLine("<table Border='0' cellpadding='1' cellspacing='1'>")

for x = 0 to UBound(Names)–1
    txtstream.WriteLine("<tr><th>" & Names(x) & "</th>")
    for y = 0 to ubound(Values) –1
        c = Rows(y)
        txtstream.WriteLine("<td>" & C(x) & "</td>")
    next
    txtstream.WriteLine("</tr>")
Next
txtstream.WriteLine("</table>")
txtstream.WriteLine("</body>")
txtstream.WriteLine("</html>")
txtstream.close
```

Text Delimited File Examples
Text files can be databases, too

Below, are code samples for creating various types of delimited files. The getValue function is in Appendix B.

Colon

```
Dim tempstr
tempstr = ""
Set ws = CreateObject("WScript.Shell")
Set fso =  CreateObject("Scripting.FileSystemObject")
Set txtstream = fso.OpenTextFile(ws.CurrentDirectory + "\Win32_Process.txt"
, 2, true, -2)
```

....

HORIZONTAL

```
For x = 0 to UBound(Names)-1
```

```
    if(tempstr <> "")
       tempstr = tempstr + ":"
    end if
    tempstr = tempstr + Names(x)
Next
txtstream.WriteLine(Tempstr)
for y = 0 to ubound(Values) -1
   C = Rows(y)
   For x = 0 to UBound(Names)-1
     if(tempstr <> "")
        tempstr = tempstr  + ":"
     end if
     tempstr = tempstr + chr(34) + C(x) + chr(34)
   Next
   txtstream.WriteLine(Tempstr)
   tempstr = ""
Next
```

VERTICAL

```
For x = 0 to UBound(Names)-1
   tempstr = Names(x)
   For y = 0 to ubound(Values) -1
     C = Rows(y)
     if(tempstr <> "")
        tempstr = tempstr  + ":"
     end if
     tempstr = tempstr + chr(34) + C(x) + chr(34)
   Next
   txtstream.WriteLine(Tempstr)
```

```
    tempstr = ""
  Next
```

Comma Delimited

```
Dim tempstr
tempstr = ""
Set ws = CreateObject("WScript.Shell")
Set fso = CreateObject("Scripting.FileSystemObject")
Set txtstream = fso.OpenTextFile(ws.CurrentDirectory + "\Win32_Process.csv"
, 2, true, -2)
```

HORIZONTAL

```
For x = 0 to UBound(Names)-1
  if(tempstr <> "")
    tempstr = tempstr + ","
  end if
  tempstr = tempstr + Names(x)
Next
txtstream.WriteLine(Tempstr)
for y = 0 to ubound(Values) -1
  C = Rows(y)
  For x = 0 to UBound(Names)-1
    if(tempstr <> "")
      tempstr = tempstr + ","
    end if
    tempstr = tempstr + chr(34) + C(x) + chr(34)
  Next
```

```
    txtstream.WriteLine(Tempstr)
    tempstr = ""
Next
```

VERTICAL

```
For x = 0 to UBound(Names)-1
   tempstr = Names(x)
   For y = 0 to ubound(Values) -1
      C = Rows(y)
      if(tempstr <> "")
         tempstr = tempstr  + ","
      end if
      tempstr = tempstr + chr(34) + C(x) + chr(34)
   Next
   txtstream.WriteLine(Tempstr)
   tempstr = ""
Next
txtstream.Close
```

Exclamation

```
Dim tempstr
tempstr = ""
Set ws = CreateObject("WScript.Shell")
Set fso =  CreateObject("Scripting.FileSystemObject")
Set txtstream = fso.OpenTextFile(ws.CurrentDirectory + "\Win32_Process.txt",
2, true, -2)
```

```
For x = 0 to UBound(Names)-1
   if(tempstr <> "")
     tempstr = tempstr + "!"
   end if
   tempstr = tempstr + Names(x)
Next
txtstream.WriteLine(Tempstr)
for y = 0 to ubound(Values) -1
   C = Rows(y)
   For x = 0 to UBound(Names)-1
     if(tempstr <> "")
       tempstr = tempstr  + "!"
     end if
     tempstr = tempstr + chr(34) + C(x) + chr(34)
   Next
   txtstream.WriteLine(Tempstr)
   tempstr = ""
Next
```

```
For x = 0 to UBound(Names)-1
   tempstr = Names(x)
   For y = 0 to ubound(Values) -1
   C = Rows(y)
```

```
        if(tempstr <> "")
           tempstr = tempstr  + "!"
        end if
        tempstr = tempstr + chr(34) + C(x) + chr(34)
     Next
     txtstream.WriteLine(Tempstr)
     tempstr = ""
  Next
```

SEMI COLON

```
Dim tempstr
tempstr = ""
Set ws = CreateObject("WScript.Shell")
Set fso =  CreateObject("Scripting.FileSystemObject")
Set txtstream = fso.OpenTextFile(ws.CurrentDirectory + "\Win32_Process.txt",
2, true, -2)
```

HORIZONTAL

```
For x = 0 to UBound(Names)-1
   if(tempstr <> "")
      tempstr = tempstr + ";"
   end if
   tempstr = tempstr + Names(x)
Next
txtstream.WriteLine(Tempstr)
```

```
for y = 0 to ubound(Values) -1
    C = Rows(y)
    For x = 0 to UBound(Names)-1
        if(tempstr <> "")
            tempstr = tempstr + ";"
        end if
        tempstr = tempstr + chr(34) + C(x) + chr(34)
    Next
    txtstream.WriteLine(Tempstr)
    tempstr = ""
Next
```

VERTICAL

```
For x = 0 to UBound(Names)-1
    tempstr = Names(x)
    For y = 0 to ubound(Values) -1
        C = Rows(y)
        if(tempstr <> "")
            tempstr = tempstr + ";"
        end if
        tempstr = tempstr + chr(34) + C(x) + chr(34)
    Next
    txtstream.WriteLine(Tempstr)
    tempstr = ""
Next
```

Tab Delimited

```
Dim tempstr
tempstr = ""
Set ws = CreateObject("WScript.Shell")
Set fso = CreateObject("Scripting.FileSystemObject")
Set txtstream = fso.OpenTextFile(ws.CurrentDirectory + "\Win32_Process.txt",
2, true, -2)
```

HORIZONTAL

```
For x = 0 to UBound(Names)-1
   if(tempstr <> "")
      tempstr = tempstr + vbtab
   end if
   tempstr = tempstr + Names(x)
Next
txtstream.WriteLine(Tempstr)
for y = 0 to ubound(Values) -1
   C = Rows(y)
   For x = 0 to UBound(Names)-1
      if(tempstr <> "")
         tempstr = tempstr  + vbtab
      end if
      tempstr = tempstr + chr(34) + C(x) + chr(34)
   Next
   txtstream.WriteLine(Tempstr)
   tempstr = ""
Next
```

```
For x = 0 to UBound(Names)-1
    tempstr = Names(x)
    For y = 0 to ubound(Values) -1
        C = Rows(y)
        if(tempstr <> "")
            tempstr = tempstr  + vbtab
        end if
        tempstr = tempstr + chr(34) + C(x) + chr(34)
    Next
    txtstream.WriteLine(Tempstr)
    tempstr = ""
Next
```

Tilde Delimited

```
Dim tempstr
tempstr = ""
Set ws = CreateObject("WScript.Shell")
Set fso = CreateObject("Scripting.FileSystemObject")
Set txtstream = fso.OpenTextFile(ws.CurrentDirectory + "\Win32_Process.txt",
2, true, -2)
```

```
For x = 0 to UBound(Names)-1
    if(tempstr <> "")
        tempstr = tempstr + "~"
    end if
    tempstr = tempstr + Names(x)
Next
txtstream.WriteLine(Tempstr)
for y = 0 to ubound(Values) -1
    C = Rows(y)
    For x = 0 to UBound(Names)-1
        if(tempstr <> "")
            tempstr = tempstr  + "~"
        end if
        tempstr = tempstr + chr(34) + C(x) + chr(34)
    Next
    txtstream.WriteLine(Tempstr)
    tempstr = ""
Next
```

VERTICAL

```
For x = 0 to UBound(Names)-1
    tempstr = Names(x)
    For y = 0 to ubound(Values) -1
        C = Rows(y)
        if(tempstr <> "~")
            tempstr = tempstr  + vbtab
        end if
        tempstr = tempstr + chr(34) + C(x) + chr(34)
```

```
        Next
        txtstream.WriteLine(Tempstr)
        tempstr = ""
    Next
```

THE XML FILES

Because they are out there

W ELL, I THOUGHT IT WAS CATCHY. Below, are examples of different types of XML that can be used with the MSDAOSP and MSPERSIST Providers. Element XML as a standalone -no XSL referenced – can be used with the MSDAOSP Provider and Schema XML can be used with MSPersist.

Element XML

```
Set ws = CreateObject("WScript.Shell")
Set    txtstream    =    fso.OpenTextFile(ws.CurrentDirectory    +
"\Win32_Process.xml", 2, true, -2)
txtstream.WriteLine("<?xml version='1.0' encoding='iso-8859-1'?>")
txtstream.WriteLine("<data>")
for y = 0 to ubound(Values) –1
   C = Rows(y)
   txtstream.WriteLine("<" + Tablename + ">")
   for x = 0 to UBound(Names)–1
      txtstream.WriteLine("<" + Names(x) + ">" + C(x) + "</" + Names(x) +
">")
      next
```

```
        txtstream.WriteLine("</" + Tablename + ">")
    next
    txtstream.WriteLine("</data>")
    txtstream.close
```

WMI to Element XML For XSL

```
    Set locator = CreateObject("WbemScripting.SWbemLocator")
    Set svc = locator.ConnectServer(".", "root\cimV2")
    svc.Security_.AuthenticationLevel=6")
    svc.Security_.ImpersonationLevel=3")
    Set ob = svc.Get("Win32_Process")
    Set objs = ob.Instances_

    Set ws = CreateObject("WScript.Shell")
    Set      txtstream      =      fso.OpenTextFile(ws.CurrentDirectory      +
"\Win32_Process.xml", 2, true, -2)
    txtstream.WriteLine("<?xml version='1.0' encoding='iso-8859-1'?>")
    txtstream.WriteLine("<?xml-stylesheet      type='Text/xsl'      href="""""      +
ws.CurrentDirectory + "\Win32_Process.xsl"""?>")
    txtstream.WriteLine("<data>")
    for y = 0 to ubound(Values) -1
      C = Rows(y)
      txtstream.WriteLine("<" + Tablename + ">")
      for x = 0 to UBound(Names)-1
        txtstream.WriteLine("<" + Names(x) + ">" + Values(y, x)+ "</" +
Names(x) + ">")
        next
        txtstream.WriteLine("</" + Tablename + ">")
    next
    txtstream.WriteLine("</data>")
    txtstream.close
```

SCHEMA XML

```
Set ws = CreateObject("WScript.Shell")
Set        txtstream        =        fso.OpenTextFile(ws.CurrentDirectory        +
"\Win32_Process.xml", 2, true, -2)
txtstream.WriteLine("<?xml version='1.0' encoding='iso-8859-1'?>")
txtstream.WriteLine("<data>")
for y = 0 to ubound(Values) -1
    C = Rows(y)
    txtstream.WriteLine("<" + Tablename + ">")
    for x = 0 to UBound(Names)-1
        txtstream.WriteLine("<" + Names(x) + ">" + Values(y, x)+ "</" +
Names(x) + ">")
        next
        txtstream.WriteLine("</" + Tablename + ">")
    next
    txtstream.WriteLine("</data>")
    txtstream.close

    Set rs1 = CreateObject("ADODB.Recordset")
    rs1.ActiveConnection          =          "Provider=MSDAOSP;        Data
Source=msxml2.DSOControl"
    rs1.Open(ws.CurrentDirectory + "\Win32_Process.xml")

    if(fso.FileExists(ws.CurrentDirectory   +   "\Win32_Process_Schema.xml")   =
true)
        fso.DeleteFile(ws.CurrentDirectory + "\Win32_Process_Schema.xml")
        end if
    rs.Save(ws.CurrentDirectory + "\Win32_Process_Schema.xml, 1)
```

EXCEL

Three ways to get the job done

THERE ARE THREE WAYS TO PUT DATA INTO EXCEL. CREATE A COMA DELIMITED FILE AND THEN USE WS.RUN, THROUGH AUTOMATION AND BY CREATING A PHYSICAL SPREADSHEET. Below are examples of doing exactly that.

Using the comma delimited file

```
Dim tempstr
tempstr = ""
Set ws = CreateObject("WScript.Shell")
Set fso = CreateObject("Scripting.FileSystemObject")
Set txtstream = fso.OpenTextFile(ws.CurrentDirectory + "\Win32_Process.csv"
, 2, true, -2)
```

HORIZONTAL

```
For x = 0 to UBound(Names)-1
```

```
    if(tempstr <> "")
        tempstr = tempstr + ","
    end if
    tempstr = tempstr + Names(x)
Next
txtstream.WriteLine(Tempstr)
for y = 0 to ubound(Values) -1
    C = Rows(y)
    For x = 0 to UBound(Names)-1
        if(tempstr <> "")
            tempstr = tempstr  + ","
        end if
        tempstr = tempstr + chr(34) + C(x) + chr(34)
    Next
    txtstream.WriteLine(Tempstr)
    tempstr = ""
Next
txtstream.close
ws.Run(ws.CurrentDirectory + "\Win32_Process.csv")
```

VERTICAL

```
For x = 0 to UBound(Names)-1
    tempstr = Names(x)
    For y = 0 to ubound(Values) -1
        C = Rows(y)
        if(tempstr <> "")
            tempstr = tempstr  + ","
        end if
        tempstr = tempstr + chr(34) + C(x) + chr(34)
```

```
        Next
        txtstream.WriteLine(Tempstr)
        tempstr = ""
    Next
    txtstream.Close

    ws.Run(ws.CurrentDirectory + "\Win32_Process.csv")
```

Excel Automation

. . . .

```
Dim x
Dim y


Set oExcel = CreateObject("Excel.Application")
oExcel.Visible = True
Set wb = oExcel.Workbooks.Add()
Set ws = wb.Worksheets(0)
ws.Name = Tablename
y=2
x=1

for x = 0 to UBound(Names)-1
    ws.Cells.Item(1, x) = Names(x)
    x=x+1
next
x=1
```

```
for y = 0 to ubound(Values) -1
  C = Rows(y)
  for x = 0 to UBound(Names)-1
    ws.Cells.Item(y, x) = Values(y, x)
    x=x+1
  next
  x= 1
  y=y+1
next
ws.Columns.HorizontalAlignment = -4131
ws.Columns.AutoFit()
```

FOR A VERTICAL VIEW

```
Dim x
Dim y

Set oExcel = CreateObject("Excel.Application")
oExcel.Visible = True
Set wb = oExcel.Workbooks.Add()
Set ws = wb.Worksheets(0)
ws.Name = Tablename
y=2
x=1

for x = 0 to UBound(Names)-1
  ws.Cells.Item(x, 1) = Names(x)
  x=x+1
next
x=1
```

```
for y = 0 to ubound(Values) -1
   C = Rows(y)
   for x = 0 to UBound(Names)-1
      ws.Cells.Item(x, y) = Values(y, x)
      x=x+1
   next
   x= 1
   y=y+1
next
ws.Columns.HorizontalAlignment = -4131
ws.Columns.AutoFit()
```

Using A Spreadsheet

```
Set locator = CreateObject("WbemScripting.SWbemLocator")
Set svc = locator.ConnectServer(".",  "root\cimV2")
svc.Security_.AuthenticationLevel=6")
svc.Security_.ImpersonationLevel=3")
Set ob = svc.Get("Win32_Process")
Set objs = ob.Instances_
```

```
Set ws = CreateObject("WScript.Shell")
Set fso = CreateObject("Scripting.FileSystemObject")
Set txtstream = fso.OpenTextFile(ws.CurrentDirectory + "\\ProcessExcel.xml",
2, True, -2)
   txtstream.WriteLine("<?xml version='1.0'?>")
   txtstream.WriteLine("<?mso-application progid='Excel.Sheet'?>")
   txtstream.WriteLine("<Workbook            xmlns='urn:schemas-microsoft-
com:office:spreadsheet'        xmlns:o='urn:schemas-microsoft-com:office:office'
xmlns:x='urn:schemas-microsoft-com:office:excel'        xmlns:ss='urn:schemas-
```

```
microsoft-com:office:spreadsheet'                xmlns:html='http://www.w3.org/TR/REC-
html40'>")
        txtstream.WriteLine("          <DocumentProperties        xmlns='urn:schemas-
microsoft-com:office:office'>")
        txtstream.WriteLine("                    <Author>Windows User</Author>")
        txtstream.WriteLine("            <LastAuthor>Windows
User</LastAuthor>")
        txtstream.WriteLine("             <Created>2007-11-
27T19:36:16Z</Created>")
        txtstream.WriteLine("              <Version>12.00</Version>")
        txtstream.WriteLine("        </DocumentProperties>")
        txtstream.WriteLine("        <ExcelWorkbook            xmlns='urn:schemas-
microsoft-com:office:excel'>")
        txtstream.WriteLine("
        <WindowHeight>11835</WindowHeight>")
        txtstream.WriteLine("
        <WindowWidth>18960</WindowWidth>")
        txtstream.WriteLine("              <WindowTopX>120</WindowTopX>")
        txtstream.WriteLine("              <WindowTopY>135</WindowTopY>")
        txtstream.WriteLine("
        <ProtectStructure>False</ProtectStructure>")
        txtstream.WriteLine("
        <ProtectWindows>False</ProtectWindows>")
        txtstream.WriteLine("         </ExcelWorkbook>")
        txtstream.WriteLine("        <Styles>")
        txtstream.WriteLine("             <Style              ss:ID='Default'
ss:Name='Normal'>")
        txtstream.WriteLine("                 <Alignment
ss:Vertical='Bottom'/>")
        txtstream.WriteLine("                 <Borders/>")
        txtstream.WriteLine("                 <Font    ss:FontName='Calibri'
x:Family='Swiss' ss:Size='11' ss:Color='#000000'/>")
        txtstream.WriteLine("                 <Interior/>")
```

```
txtstream.WriteLine("                              <NumberFormat/>")
txtstream.WriteLine("                              <Protection/>")
txtstream.WriteLine("                    </Style>")
txtstream.WriteLine("                    <Style ss:ID='s62'>")
txtstream.WriteLine("                       <Borders/>")
txtstream.WriteLine("                       <Font     ss:FontName='Calibri'
x:Family='Swiss' ss:Size='11' ss:Color='#000000' ss:Bold='1'/>")
txtstream.WriteLine("                    </Style>")
txtstream.WriteLine("                    <Style ss:ID='s63'>")
txtstream.WriteLine("                       <Alignment
ss:Horizontal='Left' ss:Vertical='Bottom' ss:Indent='2'/>")
txtstream.WriteLine("                          <Font  ss:FontName='Verdana'
x:Family='Swiss' ss:Size='7.7' ss:Color='#000000'/>")
txtstream.WriteLine("                    </Style>")
txtstream.WriteLine("  </Styles>")
txtstream.WriteLine("<Worksheet ss:Name='Process'>")
txtstream.WriteLine("             <Table    x:FullColumns='1'    x:FullRows='1'
ss:DefaultRowHeight='24.9375'>")
txtstream.WriteLine("             <Column ss:AutoFitWidth='1'  ss:Width='82.5'
ss:Span='5'/>")
For y = 0 to ubound(Values) -1
    txtstream.WriteLine("     <Row ss:AutoFitHeight='0'>")
    For x = 0 to UBound(Names)-1
        txtstream.WriteLine("                       <Cell  ss:StyleID='s62'><Data
ss:Type='String'>" + Names(x) + "</Data></Cell>")
    Next
    txtstream.WriteLine("     </Row>")
    Exit for
Next


For y = 0 to ubound(Values) -1
    C = Rows(y)
```

```
txtstream.WriteLine("        <Row ss:AutoFitHeight='0' ss:Height='13.5'>")
for x = 0 to UBound(Names)-1
    txtstream.WriteLine("            <Cell><Data ss:Type='String'><![CDATA[" +
C(x) + "]]></Data></Cell>")
Next
txtstream.WriteLine("        </Row>")
Next
txtstream.WriteLine("    </Table>")
txtstream.WriteLine("        <WorksheetOptions        xmlns='urn:schemas-
microsoft-com:office:excel'>")
txtstream.WriteLine("                    <PageSetup>")
txtstream.WriteLine("                        <Header x:Margin='0.3'/>")
txtstream.WriteLine("                        <Footer x:Margin='0.3'/>")
txtstream.WriteLine("                        <PageMargins x:Bottom='0.75'
x:Left='0.7' x:Right='0.7' x:Top='0.75'/>")
txtstream.WriteLine("                    </PageSetup>")
txtstream.WriteLine("                <Unsynced/>")
txtstream.WriteLine("                <Print>")
txtstream.WriteLine("                    <FitHeight>0</FitHeight>")
txtstream.WriteLine("                    <ValidPrinterInfo/>")
txtstream.WriteLine("
    <HorizontalResolution>600</HorizontalResolution>")
txtstream.WriteLine("
    <VerticalResolution>600</VerticalResolution>")
txtstream.WriteLine("                </Print>")
txtstream.WriteLine("                <Selected/>")
txtstream.WriteLine("                <Panes>")
txtstream.WriteLine("                    <Pane>")
txtstream.WriteLine("
    <Number>3</Number>")
txtstream.WriteLine("
    <ActiveRow>9</ActiveRow>")
```

```
txtstream.WriteLine("
    <ActiveCol>7</ActiveCol>")
txtstream.WriteLine("                                    </Pane>")
txtstream.WriteLine("                        </Panes>")
txtstream.WriteLine("
    <ProtectObjects>False</ProtectObjects>")
txtstream.WriteLine("
    <ProtectScenarios>False</ProtectScenarios>")
txtstream.WriteLine("            </WorksheetOptions>")
txtstream.WriteLine("</Worksheet>")
txtstream.WriteLine("</Workbook>")
txtstream.Close()
ws.Run(ws.CurrentDirectory + "\ProcessExcel.xml")
```

XSL

The end of the line

ELOW ARE WAYS YOU CAN CREATE XSL FILES TO RENDER YOU XML. Viewer discretion is advised.

```
Set locator = CreateObject("WbemScripting.SWbemLocator")
Set svc = locator.ConnectServer(".", "root\cimV2")
svc.Security_.AuthenticationLevel=6")
svc.Security_.ImpersonationLevel=3")
Set ob = svc.Get("Win32_Process")
Set objs = ob.Instances_
```

```
Set ws = CreateObject("WScript.Shell")
Set fso = CreateObject("Scripting.FileSystemObject")
Set txtstream = fso.OpenTextFile(ws.CurrentDirectory + "\Process.xsl", 2, true,
-2)
```

SINGLE LINE HORIZONTAL

```
txtstream.WriteLine("<?xml version=""1.0" " encoding=""UTF-8" "?>")
txtstream.WriteLine("<xsl:stylesheet                    version=""1.0""
xmlns:xsl=""http://www.w3.org/1999/XSL/Transform" ">")
txtstream.WriteLine("<xsl:template match=""/"">")
txtstream.WriteLine("<html>")
txtstream.WriteLine("<head>")
txtstream.WriteLine("<title>Products</title>")
txtstream.WriteLine("<style type='text/css'>")
txtstream.WriteLine("th")
txtstream.WriteLine("{")
txtstream.WriteLine("   COLOR: darkred;")
txtstream.WriteLine("   BACKGROUND-COLOR: white;")
txtstream.WriteLine("   FONT-FAMILY:font-family: Cambria, serif;")
txtstream.WriteLine("   FONT-SIZE: 12px;")
txtstream.WriteLine("   text-align: left;")
txtstream.WriteLine("   white-Space: nowrap;")
txtstream.WriteLine("}")
txtstream.WriteLine("td")
txtstream.WriteLine("{")
txtstream.WriteLine("   COLOR: navy;")
txtstream.WriteLine("   BACKGROUND-COLOR: white;")
txtstream.WriteLine("   FONT-FAMILY: font-family: Cambria, serif;")
txtstream.WriteLine("   FONT-SIZE: 12px;")
txtstream.WriteLine("   text-align: left;")
txtstream.WriteLine("   white-Space: nowrap;")
txtstream.WriteLine("}")
```

```
txtstream.WriteLine("</style>")
txtstream.WriteLine("</head>")
txtstream.WriteLine("<body bgcolor=""#333333" ">")
txtstream.WriteLine("<table colspacing=""3" " colpadding=""3" ">")

txtstream.WriteLine("<tr>")
for x = 0 to UBound(Names)-1
    txtstream.WriteLine("<th>" + Names(x) + </th>")
next
txtstream.WriteLine("</tr>")
txtstream.WriteLine("<tr>")
for x = 0 to UBound(Names)-1
    txtstream.WriteLine("<td><xsl:value-of  select=""data/Win32_Process/" +
Names(x)  + """/></td>")
next
txtstream.WriteLine("</tr>")
txtstream.WriteLine("</table>")
txtstream.WriteLine("</body>")
txtstream.WriteLine("</html>")
txtstream.WriteLine("</xsl:template>")
txtstream.WriteLine("</xsl:stylesheet>")
txtstream.Close()
```

For Multi Line Horizontal

```
txtstream.WriteLine("<?xml version=""1.0" " encoding=""UTF-8" "?>")
txtstream.WriteLine("<xsl:stylesheet                     version=""1.0""
xmlns:xsl=""http://www.w3.org/1999/XSL/Transform" ">")
txtstream.WriteLine("<xsl:template match=""/"">")
txtstream.WriteLine("<html>")
txtstream.WriteLine("<head>")
```

```
txtstream.WriteLine("<title>Products</title>")
txtstream.WriteLine("<style type='text/css'>")
txtstream.WriteLine("th")
txtstream.WriteLine("{")
txtstream.WriteLine("   COLOR: darkred;")
txtstream.WriteLine("   BACKGROUND-COLOR: white;")
txtstream.WriteLine("   FONT-FAMILY:font-family: Cambria, serif;")
txtstream.WriteLine("   FONT-SIZE: 12px;")
txtstream.WriteLine("   text-align: left;")
txtstream.WriteLine("   white-Space: nowrap;")
txtstream.WriteLine("}")
txtstream.WriteLine("td")
txtstream.WriteLine("{")
txtstream.WriteLine("   COLOR: navy;")
txtstream.WriteLine("   BACKGROUND-COLOR: white;")
txtstream.WriteLine("   FONT-FAMILY: font-family: Cambria, serif;")
txtstream.WriteLine("   FONT-SIZE: 12px;")
txtstream.WriteLine("   text-align: left;")
txtstream.WriteLine("   white-Space: nowrap;")
txtstream.WriteLine("}")
txtstream.WriteLine("</style>")
txtstream.WriteLine("</head>")
txtstream.WriteLine("<body bgcolor=""#333333"" ">")
txtstream.WriteLine("<table colspacing=""3"" colpadding=""3"" ">")



txtstream.WriteLine("<tr>")
for x = 0 to UBound(Names)-1
   txtstream.WriteLine("<th>" + Names(x) + </th>")
next
txtstream.WriteLine("</tr>")
txtstream.WriteLine("<xsl:for-each select=""data/Win32_Process"">")
```

```
txtstream.WriteLine("<tr>")
for x = 0 to UBound(Names)-1
    txtstream.WriteLine("<td><xsl:value-of    select=""    +    Names(x)    +
""""/></td>")
next
txtstream.WriteLine("</tr>")
txtstream.WriteLine("</xsl:for-each>")
txtstream.WriteLine("</table>")
txtstream.WriteLine("</body>")
txtstream.WriteLine("</html>")
txtstream.WriteLine("</xsl:template>")
txtstream.WriteLine("</xsl:stylesheet>")
txtstream.Close()
```

For Single Line Vertical

```
txtstream.WriteLine("<?xml version=""1.0" " encoding=""UTF-8" "?>")
txtstream.WriteLine("<xsl:stylesheet                          version=""1.0""
xmlns:xsl=""http://www.w3.org/1999/XSL/Transform" ">")
txtstream.WriteLine("<xsl:template match=""/"">")
txtstream.WriteLine("<html>")
txtstream.WriteLine("<head>")
txtstream.WriteLine("<title>Products</title>")
txtstream.WriteLine("<style type='text/css'>")
txtstream.WriteLine("th")
txtstream.WriteLine("{")
txtstream.WriteLine("   COLOR: darkred;")
txtstream.WriteLine("   BACKGROUND-COLOR: white;")
txtstream.WriteLine("   FONT-FAMILY:font-family: Cambria, serif;")
txtstream.WriteLine("   FONT-SIZE: 12px;")
txtstream.WriteLine("   text-align: left;")
txtstream.WriteLine("   white-Space: nowrap;")
```

```
txtstream.WriteLine("}")
txtstream.WriteLine("td")
txtstream.WriteLine("{")
txtstream.WriteLine("   COLOR: navy;")
txtstream.WriteLine("   BACKGROUND-COLOR: white;")
txtstream.WriteLine("   FONT-FAMILY: font-family: Cambria, serif;")
txtstream.WriteLine("   FONT-SIZE: 12px;")
txtstream.WriteLine("   text-align: left;")
txtstream.WriteLine("   white-Space: nowrap;")
txtstream.WriteLine("}")
txtstream.WriteLine("</style>")
txtstream.WriteLine("</head>")
txtstream.WriteLine("<body bgcolor=""“#333333” "">")
txtstream.WriteLine("<table colspacing=""“3” " colpadding=""“3” "">")

obj = objs.ItemIndex[0]
for x = 0 to UBound(Names)-1
    txtstream.WriteLine("<tr><th>" + Names(x) + </th>")
    txtstream.WriteLine("<td><xsl:value-of  select=""”data/Win32_Process/" + Names(x) + ""”/></td></tr>")
next
txtstream.WriteLine("</table>")
txtstream.WriteLine("</body>")
txtstream.WriteLine("</html>")
txtstream.WriteLine("</xsl:template>")
txtstream.WriteLine("</xsl:stylesheet>")
txtstream.Close()
```

For Multi Line Vertical

```
txtstream.WriteLine("<?xml version="""1.0" " encoding="""UTF-8" "?>")
txtstream.WriteLine("<xsl:stylesheet                    version="""1.0""
xmlns:xsl="""http://www.w3.org/1999/XSL/Transform" ">")
txtstream.WriteLine("<xsl:template match="""/""">")
txtstream.WriteLine("<html>")
txtstream.WriteLine("<head>")
txtstream.WriteLine("<title>Products</title>")
txtstream.WriteLine("<style type='text/css'>")
txtstream.WriteLine("th")
txtstream.WriteLine("{")
txtstream.WriteLine("    COLOR: darkred;")
txtstream.WriteLine("    BACKGROUND-COLOR: white;")
txtstream.WriteLine("    FONT-FAMILY:font-family: Cambria, serif;")
txtstream.WriteLine("    FONT-SIZE: 12px;")
txtstream.WriteLine("    text-align: left;")
txtstream.WriteLine("    white-Space: nowrap;")
txtstream.WriteLine("}")
txtstream.WriteLine("td")
txtstream.WriteLine("{")
txtstream.WriteLine("    COLOR: navy;")
txtstream.WriteLine("    BACKGROUND-COLOR: white;")
txtstream.WriteLine("    FONT-FAMILY: font-family: Cambria, serif;")
txtstream.WriteLine("    FONT-SIZE: 12px;")
txtstream.WriteLine("    text-align: left;")
txtstream.WriteLine("    white-Space: nowrap;")
txtstream.WriteLine("}")
txtstream.WriteLine("</style>")
txtstream.WriteLine("</head>")
txtstream.WriteLine("<body bgcolor="""#333333" ">")
txtstream.WriteLine("<table colspacing="""3" " colpadding="""3" ">")
```

```
txtstream.WriteLine("<tr>")
obj = objs.ItemIndex[0]
for x = 0 to UBound(Names)-1
   txtstream.WriteLine("<tr><th>" + Names(x) + </th>")
   txtstream.WriteLine("<td><xsl:for-each select=""data/Win32_Process"">")
   txtstream.WriteLine("<xsl:value-of select=""" + Names(x) + """/></td>")
   txtstream.WriteLine("</xsl:for-each></tr>")
next
txtstream.WriteLine("</table>")
txtstream.WriteLine("</body>")
txtstream.WriteLine("</html>")
txtstream.WriteLine("</xsl:template>")
txtstream.WriteLine("</xsl:stylesheet>")
txtstream.Close()
```

Stylesheets

The difference between boring and oh, wow!

The stylesheets in Appendix A, were used to render these pages. If you find one you like, feel free to use it.

Report:

Table

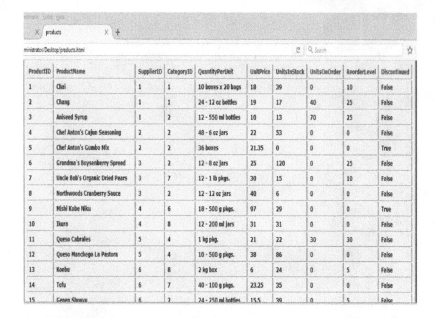

ProductID	ProductName	SupplierID	CategoryID	QuantityPerUnit	UnitPrice	UnitsInStock	UnitsOnOrder	ReorderLevel	Discontinued
1	Chai	1	1	10 boxes x 20 bags	18	39	0	10	False
2	Chang	1	1	24 - 12 oz bottles	19	17	40	25	False
3	Aniseed Syrup	1	2	12 - 550 ml bottles	10	13	70	25	False
4	Chef Anton's Cajun Seasoning	2	2	48 - 6 oz jars	22	53	0	0	False
5	Chef Anton's Gumbo Mix	2	2	36 boxes	21.35	0	0	0	True
6	Grandma's Boysenberry Spread	3	2	12 - 8 oz jars	25	120	0	25	False
7	Uncle Bob's Organic Dried Pears	3	7	12 - 1 lb pkgs.	30	15	0	10	False
8	Northwoods Cranberry Sauce	3	2	12 - 12 oz jars	40	6	0	0	False
9	Mishi Kobe Niku	4	6	18 - 500 g pkgs.	97	29	0	0	True
10	Ikura	4	8	12 - 200 ml jars	31	31	0	0	False
11	Queso Cabrales	5	4	1 kg pkg.	21	22	30	30	False
12	Queso Manchego La Pastora	5	4	10 - 500 g pkgs.	38	86	0	0	False
13	Konbu	6	8	2 kg box	6	24	0	5	False
14	Tofu	6	7	40 - 100 g pkgs.	23.25	35	0	0	False
15	Genen Shouyu	6	2	24 - 250 ml bottles	15.5	39	0	5	False

None:

Black and White

Colored:

AccountExpires	AuthorizationFlags	BadPasswordCount	Caption	CodePage	Comment	CountryCode	Description
			NT AUTHORITY\SYSTEM				Network login profile settings for SYSTEM on NT AUTHORITY
			NT AUTHORITY\LOCAL SERVICE				Network login profile settings for LOCAL SERVICE on NT AUTHORITY
			NT AUTHORITY\NETWORK SERVICE				Network login profile settings for NETWORK SERVICE on NT AUTHORITY
	0	0	Administrator	0	Built-in account for administering the computer/domain	0	Network login profile settings for on WIN-3JFLOAKMF1B
			NT SERVICE\SSASTELEMETRY				Network login profile settings for SSASTELEMETRY on NT SERVICE
			NT SERVICE\SSISTELEMETRY150				Network login profile settings for SSISTELEMETRY150 on NT SERVICE
			NT SERVICE\SQLTELEMETRY				Network login profile settings for SQLTELEMETRY on NT SERVICE
			NT SERVICE\MSSQLServerOLAPService				Network login profile settings for MSSQLServerOLAPService on NT SERVICE
			NT SERVICE\ReportServer				Network login profile settings for ReportServer on NT SERVICE
			NT SERVICE\MSSQLFDLauncher				Network login profile settings for MSSQLFDLauncher on NT SERVICE
			NT SERVICE\MSSQLLaunchpad				Network login profile settings for MSSQLLaunchpad on NT SERVICE
			NT SERVICE\SsDsServer130				Network login profile settings for SsDsServer130 on NT SERVICE
			NT SERVICE\MSSQLSERVER				Network login profile settings for MSSQLSERVER on NT SERVICE
			IIS APPPOOL\.Classic .NET AppPool				Network login profile settings for Classic .NET AppPool on IIS APPPOOL
			IIS APPPOOL\.NET v4.5				Network login profile settings for .NET v4.5 on IIS APPPOOL
			IIS APPPOOL\.NET v2.0				Network login profile settings for .NET v2.0 on IIS APPPOOL
			IIS APPPOOL\.NET v4.5 Classic				Network login profile settings for .NET v4.5 Classic on IIS APPPOOL
			IIS APPPOOL\.NET v2.0 Classic				Network login profile settings for .NET v2.0 Classic on IIS APPPOOL

Oscillating:

Availability	BytesPerSector	Capabilities	CapabilityDescriptions	Caption	CompressionMethod	ConfigManagerErrorCode	ConfigManagerUserConfig
	512	3, 4, 10	Random Access, Supports Writing, SMART Notification	OCZ REVODRIVE350 SCSI Disk Device		0	FALSE
	512	3, 4	Random Access, Supports Writing	NVMe TOSHIBA-RD400		0	FALSE
	512	3, 4, 10	Random Access, Supports Writing, SMART Notification	TOSHIBA DT01ACA200		0	FALSE

3D:

Availability	BytesPerSector	Capabilities	CapabilityDescriptions	Caption	CompressionMethod	ConfigManagerErrorCode	ConfigManagerUserConfig	CreationClassName
	512	3, 4, 10	Random Access, Supports Writing, SMART Notification	OCZ REVODRIVE350 SCSI Disk Device		0	FALSE	Win32_DiskDrive
	512	3, 4	Random Access, Supports Writing	NVMe TOSHIBA-RD400		0	FALSE	Win32_DiskDrive
	512	3, 4, 10	Random Access, Supports Writing, SMART Notification	TOSHIBA DT01ACA200		0	FALSE	Win32_DiskDrive

Shadow Box:

Availability	BytesPerSector	Capabilities	CapabilityDescriptions	Caption	CompressionMethod	ConfigManagerErrorCode	ConfigManagerUserConfig	CreationClassName	DefaultBlockSize
	512	3, 4, 10	Random Access, Supports Writing, SMART Notification	OCZ REVODRIVE350 SCSI Disk Device		0	FALSE	Win32_DiskDrive	
	512	3, 4	Random Access, Supports Writing	NVMe TOSHIBA-RD400		0	FALSE	Win32_DiskDrive	
	512	3, 4, 10	Random Access, Supports Writing, SMART Notification	TOSHIBA DT01ACA200		0	FALSE	Win32_DiskDrive	

Shadow Box Single Line Vertical

BiosCharacteristics	7, 10, 11, 12, 15, 16, 17, 19, 23, 24, 25, 26, 27, 28, 29, 32, 33, 40, 42, 43, 48, 50, 58, 59, 64, 65, 66, 67, 68, 69, 70, 71, 72, 73, 74, 75, 76, 77, 78, 79
BIOSVersion	ALASKA - 1072009, 0504, American Megatrends - 5000C
BuildNumber	
Caption	0504
CodeSet	
CurrentLanguage	en|US|iso8859-1
Description	0504
IdentificationCode	
InstallableLanguages	8
InstallDate	
LanguageEdition	
ListOfLanguages	en|US|iso8859-1, fr|FR|iso8859-1, zh|CN|unicode, , , , ,
Manufacturer	American Megatrends Inc.
Name	0504
OtherTargetOS	
PrimaryBIOS	TRUE

Shadow Box Multi line Vertical

Availability			
BytesPerSector	512	512	512
Capabilities	3, 4, 10	3, 4	3, 4, 10
CapabilityDescriptions	Random Access, Supports Writing, SMART Notification	Random Access, Supports Writing	Random Access, Supports Writing, SMART Notification
Caption	OCZ REVODRIVE350 SCSI Disk Device	NVMe TOSHIBA-RD400	TOSHIBA DT01ACA200
CompressionMethod			
ConfigManagerErrorCode	0	0	0
ConfigManagerUserConfig	FALSE	FALSE	FALSE
CreationClassName	Win32_DiskDrive	Win32_DiskDrive	Win32_DiskDrive
DefaultBlockSize			
Description	Disk drive	Disk drive	Disk drive
DeviceID	\\.\PHYSICALDRIVE2	\\.\PHYSICALDRIVE1	\\.\PHYSICALDRIVE0
ErrorCleared			
ErrorDescription			
ErrorMethodology			
FirmwareRevision	2.50	57CZ4102	MX6OABB0
Index	2	1	0

Stylesheets

Decorating your web pages

BELOW ARE SOME STYLESHEETS I COOKED UP THAT I LIKE AND THINK YOU MIGHT TOO. Don't worry I won't be offended if you take and modify to your hearts delight. Please do!

NONE

```
txtstream.WriteLine("<style type='text/css'>")
txtstream.WriteLine("th")
txtstream.WriteLine("{")
txtstream.WriteLine("   COLOR: white;")
txtstream.WriteLine("}")
txtstream.WriteLine("td")
txtstream.WriteLine("{")
txtstream.WriteLine("   COLOR: white;")
txtstream.WriteLine("}")
txtstream.WriteLine("</style>")
```

BLACK AND WHITE TEXT

```
txtstream.WriteLine("<style type='text/css'>")
txtstream.WriteLine("th")
txtstream.WriteLine("{")
txtstream.WriteLine("   COLOR: white;")
txtstream.WriteLine("   BACKGROUND-COLOR: black;")
txtstream.WriteLine("   FONT-FAMILY:font-family: Cambria, serif;")
txtstream.WriteLine("   FONT-SIZE: 12px;")
txtstream.WriteLine("   text-align: left;")
txtstream.WriteLine("   white-Space: nowrap;")
txtstream.WriteLine("}")
txtstream.WriteLine("td")
txtstream.WriteLine("{")
txtstream.WriteLine("   COLOR: white;")
txtstream.WriteLine("   BACKGROUND-COLOR: black;")
txtstream.WriteLine("   FONT-FAMILY: font-family: Cambria, serif;")
txtstream.WriteLine("   FONT-SIZE: 12px;")
txtstream.WriteLine("   text-align: left;")
txtstream.WriteLine("   white-Space: nowrap;")
txtstream.WriteLine("}")
txtstream.WriteLine("div")
txtstream.WriteLine("{")
txtstream.WriteLine("   COLOR: white;")
txtstream.WriteLine("   BACKGROUND-COLOR: black;")
txtstream.WriteLine("   FONT-FAMILY: font-family: Cambria, serif;")
txtstream.WriteLine("   FONT-SIZE: 10px;")
txtstream.WriteLine("   text-align: left;")
txtstream.WriteLine("   white-Space: nowrap;")
txtstream.WriteLine("}")
txtstream.WriteLine("span")
txtstream.WriteLine("{")
txtstream.WriteLine("   COLOR: white;")
```

```
txtstream.WriteLine("   BACKGROUND-COLOR: black;")
txtstream.WriteLine("   FONT-FAMILY: font-family: Cambria, serif;")
txtstream.WriteLine("   FONT-SIZE: 10px;")
txtstream.WriteLine("   text-align: left;")
txtstream.WriteLine("   white-Space: nowrap;")
txtstream.WriteLine("   display:inline-block;")
txtstream.WriteLine("   width: 100%;")
txtstream.WriteLine("}")
txtstream.WriteLine("textarea")
txtstream.WriteLine("{")
txtstream.WriteLine("   COLOR: white;")
txtstream.WriteLine("   BACKGROUND-COLOR: black;")
txtstream.WriteLine("   FONT-FAMILY: font-family: Cambria, serif;")
txtstream.WriteLine("   FONT-SIZE: 10px;")
txtstream.WriteLine("   text-align: left;")
txtstream.WriteLine("   white-Space: nowrap;")
txtstream.WriteLine("   width: 100%;")
txtstream.WriteLine("}")
txtstream.WriteLine("select")
txtstream.WriteLine("{")
txtstream.WriteLine("   COLOR: white;")
txtstream.WriteLine("   BACKGROUND-COLOR: black;")
txtstream.WriteLine("   FONT-FAMILY: font-family: Cambria, serif;")
txtstream.WriteLine("   FONT-SIZE: 10px;")
txtstream.WriteLine("   text-align: left;")
txtstream.WriteLine("   white-Space: nowrap;")
txtstream.WriteLine("   width: 100%;")
txtstream.WriteLine("}")
txtstream.WriteLine("input")
txtstream.WriteLine("{")
txtstream.WriteLine("   COLOR: white;")
txtstream.WriteLine("   BACKGROUND-COLOR: black;")
txtstream.WriteLine("   FONT-FAMILY: font-family: Cambria, serif;")
```

```
txtstream.WriteLine("   FONT-SIZE: 12px;")
txtstream.WriteLine("   text-align: left;")
txtstream.WriteLine("   display:table-cell;")
txtstream.WriteLine("   white-Space: nowrap;")
txtstream.WriteLine("}")
txtstream.WriteLine("h1 {")
txtstream.WriteLine("color: antiquewhite;")
txtstream.WriteLine("text-shadow: 1px 1px 1px black;")
txtstream.WriteLine("padding: 3px;")
txtstream.WriteLine("text-align: center;")
txtstream.WriteLine("box-shadow: inset 2px 2px 5px rgba(0,0,0,0.5), inset -
2px -2px 5px rgba(255,255,255,0.5);")
txtstream.WriteLine("}")
txtstream.WriteLine("</style>")
```

COLORED TEXT

```
txtstream.WriteLine("<style type='text/css'>")
txtstream.WriteLine("th")
txtstream.WriteLine("{")
txtstream.WriteLine("   COLOR: darkred;")
txtstream.WriteLine("   BACKGROUND-COLOR: #eeeeee;")
txtstream.WriteLine("   FONT-FAMILY:font-family: Cambria, serif;")
txtstream.WriteLine("   FONT-SIZE: 12px;")
txtstream.WriteLine("   text-align: left;")
txtstream.WriteLine("   white-Space: nowrap;")
txtstream.WriteLine("}")
txtstream.WriteLine("td")
txtstream.WriteLine("{")
txtstream.WriteLine("   COLOR: navy;")
txtstream.WriteLine("   BACKGROUND-COLOR: #eeeeee;")
txtstream.WriteLine("   FONT-FAMILY: font-family: Cambria, serif;")
txtstream.WriteLine("   FONT-SIZE: 12px;")
```

```
txtstream.WriteLine("    text-align: left;")
txtstream.WriteLine("    white-Space: nowrap;")
txtstream.WriteLine("}")
txtstream.WriteLine("div")
txtstream.WriteLine("{")
txtstream.WriteLine("    COLOR: white;")
txtstream.WriteLine("    BACKGROUND-COLOR: navy;")
txtstream.WriteLine("    FONT-FAMILY: font-family: Cambria, serif;")
txtstream.WriteLine("    FONT-SIZE: 10px;")
txtstream.WriteLine("    text-align: left;")
txtstream.WriteLine("    white-Space: nowrap;")
txtstream.WriteLine("}")
txtstream.WriteLine("span")
txtstream.WriteLine("{")
txtstream.WriteLine("    COLOR: white;")
txtstream.WriteLine("    BACKGROUND-COLOR: navy;")
txtstream.WriteLine("    FONT-FAMILY: font-family: Cambria, serif;")
txtstream.WriteLine("    FONT-SIZE: 10px;")
txtstream.WriteLine("    text-align: left;")
txtstream.WriteLine("    white-Space: nowrap;")
txtstream.WriteLine("    display:inline-block;")
txtstream.WriteLine("    width: 100%;")
txtstream.WriteLine("}")
txtstream.WriteLine("textarea")
txtstream.WriteLine("{")
txtstream.WriteLine("    COLOR: white;")
txtstream.WriteLine("    BACKGROUND-COLOR: navy;")
txtstream.WriteLine("    FONT-FAMILY: font-family: Cambria, serif;")
txtstream.WriteLine("    FONT-SIZE: 10px;")
txtstream.WriteLine("    text-align: left;")
txtstream.WriteLine("    white-Space: nowrap;")
txtstream.WriteLine("    width: 100%;")
txtstream.WriteLine("}")
```

```
txtstream.WriteLine("select")
txtstream.WriteLine("{")
txtstream.WriteLine("    COLOR: white;")
txtstream.WriteLine("    BACKGROUND-COLOR: navy;")
txtstream.WriteLine("    FONT-FAMILY: font-family: Cambria, serif;")
txtstream.WriteLine("    FONT-SIZE: 10px;")
txtstream.WriteLine("    text-align: left;")
txtstream.WriteLine("    white-Space: nowrap;")
txtstream.WriteLine("    width: 100%;")
txtstream.WriteLine("}")
txtstream.WriteLine("input")
txtstream.WriteLine("{")
txtstream.WriteLine("    COLOR: white;")
txtstream.WriteLine("    BACKGROUND-COLOR: navy;")
txtstream.WriteLine("    FONT-FAMILY: font-family: Cambria, serif;")
txtstream.WriteLine("    FONT-SIZE: 12px;")
txtstream.WriteLine("    text-align: left;")
txtstream.WriteLine("    display:table-cell;")
txtstream.WriteLine("    white-Space: nowrap;")
txtstream.WriteLine("}")
txtstream.WriteLine("h1 {")
txtstream.WriteLine("color: antiquewhite;")
txtstream.WriteLine("text-shadow: 1px 1px 1px black;")
txtstream.WriteLine("padding: 3px;")
txtstream.WriteLine("text-align: center;")
txtstream.WriteLine("box-shadow: inset 2px 2px 5px rgba(0,0,0,0.5), inset
2px -2px 5px rgba(255,255,255,0.5);")
txtstream.WriteLine("}")
txtstream.WriteLine("</style>")
```

OSCILLATING ROW COLORS

```
txtstream.WriteLine("<style>")
txtstream.WriteLine("th")
txtstream.WriteLine("{")
txtstream.WriteLine("    COLOR: white;")
txtstream.WriteLine("    BACKGROUND-COLOR: navy;")
txtstream.WriteLine("    FONT-FAMILY:font-family: Cambria, serif;")
txtstream.WriteLine("    FONT-SIZE: 12px;")
txtstream.WriteLine("    text-align: left;")
txtstream.WriteLine("    white-Space: nowrap;")
txtstream.WriteLine("}")
txtstream.WriteLine("td")
txtstream.WriteLine("{")
txtstream.WriteLine("    COLOR: navy;")
txtstream.WriteLine("    FONT-FAMILY: font-family: Cambria, serif;")
txtstream.WriteLine("    FONT-SIZE: 12px;")
txtstream.WriteLine("    text-align: left;")
txtstream.WriteLine("    white-Space: nowrap;")
txtstream.WriteLine("}")
txtstream.WriteLine("div")
txtstream.WriteLine("{")
txtstream.WriteLine("    COLOR: navy;")
txtstream.WriteLine("    FONT-FAMILY: font-family: Cambria, serif;")
txtstream.WriteLine("    FONT-SIZE: 12px;")
txtstream.WriteLine("    text-align: left;")
txtstream.WriteLine("    white-Space: nowrap;")
txtstream.WriteLine("}")
txtstream.WriteLine("span")
txtstream.WriteLine("{")
txtstream.WriteLine("    COLOR: navy;")
txtstream.WriteLine("    FONT-FAMILY: font-family: Cambria, serif;")
txtstream.WriteLine("    FONT-SIZE: 12px;")
txtstream.WriteLine("    text-align: left;")
```

```
txtstream.WriteLine("    white-Space: nowrap;")
txtstream.WriteLine("    width: 100%;")
txtstream.WriteLine("}")
txtstream.WriteLine("textarea")
txtstream.WriteLine("{")
txtstream.WriteLine("    COLOR: navy;")
txtstream.WriteLine("    FONT-FAMILY: font-family: Cambria, serif;")
txtstream.WriteLine("    FONT-SIZE: 12px;")
txtstream.WriteLine("    text-align: left;")
txtstream.WriteLine("    white-Space: nowrap;")
txtstream.WriteLine("    display:inline-block;")
txtstream.WriteLine("    width: 100%;")
txtstream.WriteLine("}")
txtstream.WriteLine("select")
txtstream.WriteLine("{")
txtstream.WriteLine("    COLOR: navy;")
txtstream.WriteLine("    FONT-FAMILY: font-family: Cambria, serif;")
txtstream.WriteLine("    FONT-SIZE: 10px;")
txtstream.WriteLine("    text-align: left;")
txtstream.WriteLine("    white-Space: nowrap;")
txtstream.WriteLine("    display:inline-block;")
txtstream.WriteLine("    width: 100%;")
txtstream.WriteLine("}")
txtstream.WriteLine("input")
txtstream.WriteLine("{")
txtstream.WriteLine("    COLOR: navy;")
txtstream.WriteLine("    FONT-FAMILY: font-family: Cambria, serif;")
txtstream.WriteLine("    FONT-SIZE: 12px;")
txtstream.WriteLine("    text-align: left;")
txtstream.WriteLine("    display:table-cell;")
txtstream.WriteLine("    white-Space: nowrap;")
txtstream.WriteLine("}")
txtstream.WriteLine("h1 {")
```

```
txtstream.WriteLine("color: antiquewhite;")
txtstream.WriteLine("text-shadow: 1px 1px 1px black;")
txtstream.WriteLine("padding: 3px;")
txtstream.WriteLine("text-align: center;")
txtstream.WriteLine("box-shadow: inset 2px 2px 5px rgba(0,0,0,0.5), inset -
2px -2px 5px rgba(255,255,255,0.5);")
txtstream.WriteLine("}")
txtstream.WriteLine("tr:nth-child(even){background-color:#f2f2f2;}")
txtstream.WriteLine("tr:nth-child(odd){background-color:#cccccc;
color:#f2f2f2;}")
txtstream.WriteLine("</style>")
```

GHOST DECORATED

```
txtstream.WriteLine("<style type='text/css'>")
txtstream.WriteLine("th")
txtstream.WriteLine("{")
txtstream.WriteLine("    COLOR: black;")
txtstream.WriteLine("    BACKGROUND-COLOR: white;")
txtstream.WriteLine("    FONT-FAMILY:font-family: Cambria, serif;")
txtstream.WriteLine("    FONT-SIZE: 12px;")
txtstream.WriteLine("    text-align: left;")
txtstream.WriteLine("    white-Space: nowrap;")
txtstream.WriteLine("}")
txtstream.WriteLine("td")
txtstream.WriteLine("{")
txtstream.WriteLine("    COLOR: black;")
txtstream.WriteLine("    BACKGROUND-COLOR: white;")
txtstream.WriteLine("    FONT-FAMILY: font-family: Cambria, serif;")
txtstream.WriteLine("    FONT-SIZE: 12px;")
txtstream.WriteLine("    text-align: left;")
txtstream.WriteLine("    white-Space: nowrap;")
txtstream.WriteLine("}")
```

```
txtstream.WriteLine("div")
txtstream.WriteLine("{")
txtstream.WriteLine("   COLOR: black;")
txtstream.WriteLine("   BACKGROUND-COLOR: white;")
txtstream.WriteLine("   FONT-FAMILY: font-family: Cambria, serif;")
txtstream.WriteLine("   FONT-SIZE: 10px;")
txtstream.WriteLine("   text-align: left;")
txtstream.WriteLine("   white-Space: nowrap;")
txtstream.WriteLine("}")
txtstream.WriteLine("span")
txtstream.WriteLine("{")
txtstream.WriteLine("   COLOR: black;")
txtstream.WriteLine("   BACKGROUND-COLOR: white;")
txtstream.WriteLine("   FONT-FAMILY: font-family: Cambria, serif;")
txtstream.WriteLine("   FONT-SIZE: 10px;")
txtstream.WriteLine("   text-align: left;")
txtstream.WriteLine("   white-Space: nowrap;")
txtstream.WriteLine("   display:inline-block;")
txtstream.WriteLine("   width: 100%;")
txtstream.WriteLine("}")
txtstream.WriteLine("textarea")
txtstream.WriteLine("{")
txtstream.WriteLine("   COLOR: black;")
txtstream.WriteLine("   BACKGROUND-COLOR: white;")
txtstream.WriteLine("   FONT-FAMILY: font-family: Cambria, serif;")
txtstream.WriteLine("   FONT-SIZE: 10px;")
txtstream.WriteLine("   text-align: left;")
txtstream.WriteLine("   white-Space: nowrap;")
txtstream.WriteLine("   width: 100%;")
txtstream.WriteLine("}")
txtstream.WriteLine("select")
txtstream.WriteLine("{")
txtstream.WriteLine("   COLOR: black;")
```

```
txtstream.WriteLine("    BACKGROUND-COLOR: white;")
txtstream.WriteLine("    FONT-FAMILY: font-family: Cambria, serif;")
txtstream.WriteLine("    FONT-SIZE: 10px;")
txtstream.WriteLine("    text-align: left;")
txtstream.WriteLine("    white-Space: nowrap;")
txtstream.WriteLine("    width: 100%;")
txtstream.WriteLine("}")
txtstream.WriteLine("input")
txtstream.WriteLine("{")
txtstream.WriteLine("    COLOR: black;")
txtstream.WriteLine("    BACKGROUND-COLOR: white;")
txtstream.WriteLine("    FONT-FAMILY: font-family: Cambria, serif;")
txtstream.WriteLine("    FONT-SIZE: 12px;")
txtstream.WriteLine("    text-align: left;")
txtstream.WriteLine("    display:table-cell;")
txtstream.WriteLine("    white-Space: nowrap;")
txtstream.WriteLine("}")
txtstream.WriteLine("h1 {")
txtstream.WriteLine("color: antiquewhite;")
txtstream.WriteLine("text-shadow: 1px 1px 1px black;")
txtstream.WriteLine("padding: 3px;")
txtstream.WriteLine("text-align: center;")
txtstream.WriteLine("box-shadow: inset 2px 2px 5px rgba(0,0,0,0.5), inset -2px -2px 5px rgba(255,255,255,0.5);")
txtstream.WriteLine("}")
txtstream.WriteLine("</style>")
```

3D

```
txtstream.WriteLine("<style type='text/css'>")
txtstream.WriteLine("body")
txtstream.WriteLine("{")
```

```
txtstream.WriteLine("    PADDING-RIGHT: 0px;")
txtstream.WriteLine("    PADDING-LEFT: 0px;")
txtstream.WriteLine("    PADDING-BOTTOM: 0px;")
txtstream.WriteLine("    MARGIN: 0px;")
txtstream.WriteLine("    COLOR: #333;")
txtstream.WriteLine("    PADDING-TOP: 0px;")
txtstream.WriteLine("    FONT-FAMILY: verdana, arial, helvetica, sans-serif;")
txtstream.WriteLine("}")
txtstream.WriteLine("table")
txtstream.WriteLine("{")
txtstream.WriteLine("    BORDER-RIGHT: #999999 3px solid;")
txtstream.WriteLine("    PADDING-RIGHT: 6px;")
txtstream.WriteLine("    PADDING-LEFT: 6px;")
txtstream.WriteLine("    FONT-WEIGHT: Bold;")
txtstream.WriteLine("    FONT-SIZE: 14px;")
txtstream.WriteLine("    PADDING-BOTTOM: 6px;")
txtstream.WriteLine("    COLOR: Peru;")
txtstream.WriteLine("    LINE-HEIGHT: 14px;")
txtstream.WriteLine("    PADDING-TOP: 6px;")
txtstream.WriteLine("    BORDER-BOTTOM: #999 1px solid;")
txtstream.WriteLine("    BACKGROUND-COLOR: #eeeeee;")
txtstream.WriteLine("    FONT-FAMILY: verdana, arial, helvetica, sans-serif;")
txtstream.WriteLine("    FONT-SIZE: 12px;")
txtstream.WriteLine("}")
txtstream.WriteLine("th")
txtstream.WriteLine("{")
txtstream.WriteLine("    BORDER-RIGHT: #999999 3px solid;")
txtstream.WriteLine("    PADDING-RIGHT: 6px;")
txtstream.WriteLine("    PADDING-LEFT: 6px;")
txtstream.WriteLine("    FONT-WEIGHT: Bold;")
txtstream.WriteLine("    FONT-SIZE: 14px;")
txtstream.WriteLine("    PADDING-BOTTOM: 6px;")
txtstream.WriteLine("    COLOR: darkred;")
```

```
txtstream.WriteLine("    LINE-HEIGHT: 14px;")
txtstream.WriteLine("    PADDING-TOP: 6px;")
txtstream.WriteLine("    BORDER-BOTTOM: #999 1px solid;")
txtstream.WriteLine("    BACKGROUND-COLOR: #eeeeee;")
txtstream.WriteLine("    FONT-FAMILY:font-family: Cambria, serif;")
txtstream.WriteLine("    FONT-SIZE: 12px;")
txtstream.WriteLine("    text-align: left;")
txtstream.WriteLine("    white-Space: nowrap;")
txtstream.WriteLine("}")
txtstream.WriteLine(".th")
txtstream.WriteLine("{")
txtstream.WriteLine("    BORDER-RIGHT: #999999 2px solid;")
txtstream.WriteLine("    PADDING-RIGHT: 6px;")
txtstream.WriteLine("    PADDING-LEFT: 6px;")
txtstream.WriteLine("    FONT-WEIGHT: Bold;")
txtstream.WriteLine("    PADDING-BOTTOM: 6px;")
txtstream.WriteLine("    COLOR: black;")
txtstream.WriteLine("    PADDING-TOP: 6px;")
txtstream.WriteLine("    BORDER-BOTTOM: #999 2px solid;")
txtstream.WriteLine("    BACKGROUND-COLOR: #eeeeee;")
txtstream.WriteLine("    FONT-FAMILY: font-family: Cambria, serif;")
txtstream.WriteLine("    FONT-SIZE: 10px;")
txtstream.WriteLine("    text-align: right;")
txtstream.WriteLine("    white-Space: nowrap;")
txtstream.WriteLine("}")
txtstream.WriteLine("td")
txtstream.WriteLine("{")
txtstream.WriteLine("    BORDER-RIGHT: #999999 3px solid;")
txtstream.WriteLine("    PADDING-RIGHT: 6px;")
txtstream.WriteLine("    PADDING-LEFT: 6px;")
txtstream.WriteLine("    FONT-WEIGHT: Normal;")
txtstream.WriteLine("    PADDING-BOTTOM: 6px;")
txtstream.WriteLine("    COLOR: navy;")
```

```
txtstream.WriteLine("    LINE-HEIGHT: 14px;")
txtstream.WriteLine("    PADDING-TOP: 6px;")
txtstream.WriteLine("    BORDER-BOTTOM: #999 1px solid;")
txtstream.WriteLine("    BACKGROUND-COLOR: #eeeeee;")
txtstream.WriteLine("    FONT-FAMILY: font-family: Cambria, serif;")
txtstream.WriteLine("    FONT-SIZE: 12px;")
txtstream.WriteLine("    text-align: left;")
txtstream.WriteLine("    white-Space: nowrap;")
txtstream.WriteLine("}")
txtstream.WriteLine("div")
txtstream.WriteLine("{")
txtstream.WriteLine("    BORDER-RIGHT: #999999 3px solid;")
txtstream.WriteLine("    PADDING-RIGHT: 6px;")
txtstream.WriteLine("    PADDING-LEFT: 6px;")
txtstream.WriteLine("    FONT-WEIGHT: Normal;")
txtstream.WriteLine("    PADDING-BOTTOM: 6px;")
txtstream.WriteLine("    COLOR: white;")
txtstream.WriteLine("    PADDING-TOP: 6px;")
txtstream.WriteLine("    BORDER-BOTTOM: #999 1px solid;")
txtstream.WriteLine("    BACKGROUND-COLOR: navy;")
txtstream.WriteLine("    FONT-FAMILY: font-family: Cambria, serif;")
txtstream.WriteLine("    FONT-SIZE: 10px;")
txtstream.WriteLine("    text-align: left;")
txtstream.WriteLine("    white-Space: nowrap;")
txtstream.WriteLine("}")
txtstream.WriteLine("span")
txtstream.WriteLine("{")
txtstream.WriteLine("    BORDER-RIGHT: #999999 3px solid;")
txtstream.WriteLine("    PADDING-RIGHT: 3px;")
txtstream.WriteLine("    PADDING-LEFT: 3px;")
txtstream.WriteLine("    FONT-WEIGHT: Normal;")
txtstream.WriteLine("    PADDING-BOTTOM: 3px;")
txtstream.WriteLine("    COLOR: white;")
```

```
txtstream.WriteLine("   PADDING-TOP: 3px;")
txtstream.WriteLine("   BORDER-BOTTOM: #999 1px solid;")
txtstream.WriteLine("   BACKGROUND-COLOR: navy;")
txtstream.WriteLine("   FONT-FAMILY: font-family: Cambria, serif;")
txtstream.WriteLine("   FONT-SIZE: 10px;")
txtstream.WriteLine("   text-align: left;")
txtstream.WriteLine("   white-Space: nowrap;")
txtstream.WriteLine("   display:inline-block;")
txtstream.WriteLine("   width: 100%;")
txtstream.WriteLine("}")
txtstream.WriteLine("textarea")
txtstream.WriteLine("{")
txtstream.WriteLine("   BORDER-RIGHT: #999999 3px solid;")
txtstream.WriteLine("   PADDING-RIGHT: 3px;")
txtstream.WriteLine("   PADDING-LEFT: 3px;")
txtstream.WriteLine("   FONT-WEIGHT: Normal;")
txtstream.WriteLine("   PADDING-BOTTOM: 3px;")
txtstream.WriteLine("   COLOR: white;")
txtstream.WriteLine("   PADDING-TOP: 3px;")
txtstream.WriteLine("   BORDER-BOTTOM: #999 1px solid;")
txtstream.WriteLine("   BACKGROUND-COLOR: navy;")
txtstream.WriteLine("   FONT-FAMILY: font-family: Cambria, serif;")
txtstream.WriteLine("   FONT-SIZE: 10px;")
txtstream.WriteLine("   text-align: left;")
txtstream.WriteLine("   white-Space: nowrap;")
txtstream.WriteLine("   width: 100%;")
txtstream.WriteLine("}")
txtstream.WriteLine("select")
txtstream.WriteLine("{")
txtstream.WriteLine("   BORDER-RIGHT: #999999 3px solid;")
txtstream.WriteLine("   PADDING-RIGHT: 6px;")
txtstream.WriteLine("   PADDING-LEFT: 6px;")
txtstream.WriteLine("   FONT-WEIGHT: Normal;")
```

```
txtstream.WriteLine("    PADDING-BOTTOM: 6px;")
txtstream.WriteLine("    COLOR: white;")
txtstream.WriteLine("    PADDING-TOP: 6px;")
txtstream.WriteLine("    BORDER-BOTTOM: #999 1px solid;")
txtstream.WriteLine("    BACKGROUND-COLOR: navy;")
txtstream.WriteLine("    FONT-FAMILY: font-family: Cambria, serif;")
txtstream.WriteLine("    FONT-SIZE: 10px;")
txtstream.WriteLine("    text-align: left;")
txtstream.WriteLine("    white-Space: nowrap;")
txtstream.WriteLine("    width: 100%;")
txtstream.WriteLine("}")
txtstream.WriteLine("input")
txtstream.WriteLine("{")
txtstream.WriteLine("    BORDER-RIGHT: #999999 3px solid;")
txtstream.WriteLine("    PADDING-RIGHT: 3px;")
txtstream.WriteLine("    PADDING-LEFT: 3px;")
txtstream.WriteLine("    FONT-WEIGHT: Bold;")
txtstream.WriteLine("    PADDING-BOTTOM: 3px;")
txtstream.WriteLine("    COLOR: white;")
txtstream.WriteLine("    PADDING-TOP: 3px;")
txtstream.WriteLine("    BORDER-BOTTOM: #999 1px solid;")
txtstream.WriteLine("    BACKGROUND-COLOR: navy;")
txtstream.WriteLine("    FONT-FAMILY: font-family: Cambria, serif;")
txtstream.WriteLine("    FONT-SIZE: 12px;")
txtstream.WriteLine("    text-align: left;")
txtstream.WriteLine("    display:table-cell;")
txtstream.WriteLine("    white-Space: nowrap;")
txtstream.WriteLine("    width: 100%;")
txtstream.WriteLine("}")
txtstream.WriteLine("h1 {")
txtstream.WriteLine("color: antiquewhite;")
txtstream.WriteLine("text-shadow: 1px 1px 1px black;")
txtstream.WriteLine("padding: 3px;")
```

```
txtstream.WriteLine("text-align: center;")
txtstream.WriteLine("box-shadow: inset 2px 2px 5px rgba(0,0,0,0.5), inset -
2px -2px 5px rgba(255,255,255,0.5);")
txtstream.WriteLine("}")
txtstream.WriteLine("</style>")
```

SHADOW BOX

```
txtstream.WriteLine("<style type='text/css'>")
txtstream.WriteLine("body")
txtstream.WriteLine("{")
txtstream.WriteLine("   PADDING-RIGHT: 0px;")
txtstream.WriteLine("   PADDING-LEFT: 0px;")
txtstream.WriteLine("   PADDING-BOTTOM: 0px;")
txtstream.WriteLine("   MARGIN: 0px;")
txtstream.WriteLine("   COLOR: #333;")
txtstream.WriteLine("   PADDING-TOP: 0px;")
txtstream.WriteLine("   FONT-FAMILY: verdana, arial, helvetica, sans-serif;")
txtstream.WriteLine("}")
txtstream.WriteLine("table")
txtstream.WriteLine("{")
txtstream.WriteLine("   BORDER-RIGHT: #999999 1px solid;")
txtstream.WriteLine("   PADDING-RIGHT: 1px;")
txtstream.WriteLine("   PADDING-LEFT: 1px;")
txtstream.WriteLine("   PADDING-BOTTOM: 1px;")
txtstream.WriteLine("   LINE-HEIGHT: 8px;")
txtstream.WriteLine("   PADDING-TOP: 1px;")
txtstream.WriteLine("   BORDER-BOTTOM: #999 1px solid;")
txtstream.WriteLine("   BACKGROUND-COLOR: #eeeeee;")
txtstream.WriteLine("
filter:progid:DXImageTransform.Microsoft.Shadow(color='silver',     Direction=135,
Strength=16)")
txtstream.WriteLine("}")
```

```
txtstream.WriteLine("th")
txtstream.WriteLine("{")
txtstream.WriteLine("    BORDER-RIGHT: #999999 3px solid;")
txtstream.WriteLine("    PADDING-RIGHT: 6px;")
txtstream.WriteLine("    PADDING-LEFT: 6px;")
txtstream.WriteLine("    FONT-WEIGHT: Bold;")
txtstream.WriteLine("    FONT-SIZE: 14px;")
txtstream.WriteLine("    PADDING-BOTTOM: 6px;")
txtstream.WriteLine("    COLOR: darkred;")
txtstream.WriteLine("    LINE-HEIGHT: 14px;")
txtstream.WriteLine("    PADDING-TOP: 6px;")
txtstream.WriteLine("    BORDER-BOTTOM: #999 1px solid;")
txtstream.WriteLine("    BACKGROUND-COLOR: #eeeeee;")
txtstream.WriteLine("    FONT-FAMILY: font-family: Cambria, serif;")
txtstream.WriteLine("    FONT-SIZE: 12px;")
txtstream.WriteLine("    text-align: left;")
txtstream.WriteLine("    white-Space: nowrap;")
txtstream.WriteLine("}")
txtstream.WriteLine(".th")
txtstream.WriteLine("{")
txtstream.WriteLine("    BORDER-RIGHT: #999999 2px solid;")
txtstream.WriteLine("    PADDING-RIGHT: 6px;")
txtstream.WriteLine("    PADDING-LEFT: 6px;")
txtstream.WriteLine("    FONT-WEIGHT: Bold;")
txtstream.WriteLine("    PADDING-BOTTOM: 6px;")
txtstream.WriteLine("    COLOR: black;")
txtstream.WriteLine("    PADDING-TOP: 6px;")
txtstream.WriteLine("    BORDER-BOTTOM: #999 2px solid;")
txtstream.WriteLine("    BACKGROUND-COLOR: #eeeeee;")
txtstream.WriteLine("    FONT-FAMILY: font-family: Cambria, serif;")
txtstream.WriteLine("    FONT-SIZE: 10px;")
txtstream.WriteLine("    text-align: right;")
txtstream.WriteLine("    white-Space: nowrap;")
```

```
txtstream.WriteLine("}")
txtstream.WriteLine("td")
txtstream.WriteLine("{")
txtstream.WriteLine("   BORDER-RIGHT: #999999 3px solid;")
txtstream.WriteLine("   PADDING-RIGHT: 6px;")
txtstream.WriteLine("   PADDING-LEFT: 6px;")
txtstream.WriteLine("   FONT-WEIGHT: Normal;")
txtstream.WriteLine("   PADDING-BOTTOM: 6px;")
txtstream.WriteLine("   COLOR: navy;")
txtstream.WriteLine("   LINE-HEIGHT: 14px;")
txtstream.WriteLine("   PADDING-TOP: 6px;")
txtstream.WriteLine("   BORDER-BOTTOM: #999 1px solid;")
txtstream.WriteLine("   BACKGROUND-COLOR: #eeeeee;")
txtstream.WriteLine("   FONT-FAMILY: font-family: Cambria, serif;")
txtstream.WriteLine("   FONT-SIZE: 12px;")
txtstream.WriteLine("   text-align: left;")
txtstream.WriteLine("   white-Space: nowrap;")
txtstream.WriteLine("}")
txtstream.WriteLine("div")
txtstream.WriteLine("{")
txtstream.WriteLine("   BORDER-RIGHT: #999999 3px solid;")
txtstream.WriteLine("   PADDING-RIGHT: 6px;")
txtstream.WriteLine("   PADDING-LEFT: 6px;")
txtstream.WriteLine("   FONT-WEIGHT: Normal;")
txtstream.WriteLine("   PADDING-BOTTOM: 6px;")
txtstream.WriteLine("   COLOR: white;")
txtstream.WriteLine("   PADDING-TOP: 6px;")
txtstream.WriteLine("   BORDER-BOTTOM: #999 1px solid;")
txtstream.WriteLine("   BACKGROUND-COLOR: navy;")
txtstream.WriteLine("   FONT-FAMILY: font-family: Cambria, serif;")
txtstream.WriteLine("   FONT-SIZE: 10px;")
txtstream.WriteLine("   text-align: left;")
txtstream.WriteLine("   white-Space: nowrap;")
```

```
txtstream.WriteLine("}")
txtstream.WriteLine("span")
txtstream.WriteLine("{")
txtstream.WriteLine("    BORDER-RIGHT: #999999 3px solid;")
txtstream.WriteLine("    PADDING-RIGHT: 3px;")
txtstream.WriteLine("    PADDING-LEFT: 3px;")
txtstream.WriteLine("    FONT-WEIGHT: Normal;")
txtstream.WriteLine("    PADDING-BOTTOM: 3px;")
txtstream.WriteLine("    COLOR: white;")
txtstream.WriteLine("    PADDING-TOP: 3px;")
txtstream.WriteLine("    BORDER-BOTTOM: #999 1px solid;")
txtstream.WriteLine("    BACKGROUND-COLOR: navy;")
txtstream.WriteLine("    FONT-FAMILY: font-family: Cambria, serif;")
txtstream.WriteLine("    FONT-SIZE: 10px;")
txtstream.WriteLine("    text-align: left;")
txtstream.WriteLine("    white-Space: nowrap;")
txtstream.WriteLine("    display: inline-block;")
txtstream.WriteLine("    width: 100%;")
txtstream.WriteLine("}")
txtstream.WriteLine("textarea")
txtstream.WriteLine("{")
txtstream.WriteLine("    BORDER-RIGHT: #999999 3px solid;")
txtstream.WriteLine("    PADDING-RIGHT: 3px;")
txtstream.WriteLine("    PADDING-LEFT: 3px;")
txtstream.WriteLine("    FONT-WEIGHT: Normal;")
txtstream.WriteLine("    PADDING-BOTTOM: 3px;")
txtstream.WriteLine("    COLOR: white;")
txtstream.WriteLine("    PADDING-TOP: 3px;")
txtstream.WriteLine("    BORDER-BOTTOM: #999 1px solid;")
txtstream.WriteLine("    BACKGROUND-COLOR: navy;")
txtstream.WriteLine("    FONT-FAMILY: font-family: Cambria, serif;")
txtstream.WriteLine("    FONT-SIZE: 10px;")
txtstream.WriteLine("    text-align: left;")
```

```
txtstream.WriteLine("    white-Space: nowrap;")
txtstream.WriteLine("    width: 100%;")
txtstream.WriteLine("}")
txtstream.WriteLine("select")
txtstream.WriteLine("{")
txtstream.WriteLine("    BORDER-RIGHT: #999999 3px solid;")
txtstream.WriteLine("    PADDING-RIGHT: 6px;")
txtstream.WriteLine("    PADDING-LEFT: 6px;")
txtstream.WriteLine("    FONT-WEIGHT: Normal;")
txtstream.WriteLine("    PADDING-BOTTOM: 6px;")
txtstream.WriteLine("    COLOR: white;")
txtstream.WriteLine("    PADDING-TOP: 6px;")
txtstream.WriteLine("    BORDER-BOTTOM: #999 1px solid;")
txtstream.WriteLine("    BACKGROUND-COLOR: navy;")
txtstream.WriteLine("    FONT-FAMILY: font-family: Cambria, serif;")
txtstream.WriteLine("    FONT-SIZE: 10px;")
txtstream.WriteLine("    text-align: left;")
txtstream.WriteLine("    white-Space: nowrap;")
txtstream.WriteLine("    width: 100%;")
txtstream.WriteLine("}")
txtstream.WriteLine("input")
txtstream.WriteLine("{")
txtstream.WriteLine("    BORDER-RIGHT: #999999 3px solid;")
txtstream.WriteLine("    PADDING-RIGHT: 3px;")
txtstream.WriteLine("    PADDING-LEFT: 3px;")
txtstream.WriteLine("    FONT-WEIGHT: Bold;")
txtstream.WriteLine("    PADDING-BOTTOM: 3px;")
txtstream.WriteLine("    COLOR: white;")
txtstream.WriteLine("    PADDING-TOP: 3px;")
txtstream.WriteLine("    BORDER-BOTTOM: #999 1px solid;")
txtstream.WriteLine("    BACKGROUND-COLOR: navy;")
txtstream.WriteLine("    FONT-FAMILY: font-family: Cambria, serif;")
txtstream.WriteLine("    FONT-SIZE: 12px;")
```

```
txtstream.WriteLine("    text-align: left;")
txtstream.WriteLine("    display: table-cell;")
txtstream.WriteLine("    white-Space: nowrap;")
txtstream.WriteLine("    width: 100%;")
txtstream.WriteLine("}")
txtstream.WriteLine("h1 {")
txtstream.WriteLine("color: antiquewhite;")
txtstream.WriteLine("text-shadow: 1px 1px 1px black;")
txtstream.WriteLine("padding: 3px;")
txtstream.WriteLine("text-align: center;")
txtstream.WriteLine("box-shadow: inset 2px 2px 5px rgba(0,0,0,0.5), inset -2px -2px 5px rgba(255,255,255,0.5);")
txtstream.WriteLine("}")
txtstream.WriteLine("</style>")
```

Appendix B
The GetValue routine

Chapter Epigraph uses a quote or verse to
introduce the chapter and set the stage.
—Attribute the quote

SPECIFICALLY PLACED THIS HERE BECAUSE THE ROUTE TAKES UP AROUND 30 OF THIS BOOK AND I WANTED TO REPLACE IT WITH SOME STYLESHEET BEAUTIFICATION OF THE EXAMPLES.

```
Function GetValue(ByVal Name, ByVal obj)

  Dim tempstr, pos, pName
  pName = Name
  tempstr = obj.GetObjectText_
  Name = Name + " = "
  pos = InStr(tempstr, Name)
  if pos Then
    pos = pos + Len(Name)
```

```
        tempstr = Mid(tempstr, pos, Len(tempstr))
        pos = InStr(tempstr, ";")
        tempstr = Mid(tempstr, 1, pos - 1)
        tempstr = Replace(tempstr, Chr(34), "")
        tempstr = Replace(tempstr, "{", "")
        tempstr = Replace(tempstr, "}", "")
        tempstr = Trim(tempstr)
        if obj.Properties_(pName).CIMType = 101 Then
            tempstr = Mid(tempstr, 5, 2) + "/" + _
            Mid(tempstr, 7, 2) + "/" + _
            Mid(tempstr, 1, 4) + " " + _
            Mid(tempstr, 9, 2) + ":" + _
            Mid(tempstr, 11, 2) + ":" + _
            Mid(tempstr, 13, 2)
        End If
    GetValue = tempstr
    Else
    GetValue = ""
    End If


End Function
```

www.ingramcontent.com/pod-product-compliance
Lightning Source LLC
Chambersburg PA
CBHW071550080326
40690CB00056B/1616